THE FUTURE of COMMUNITY BROADCAST TELEVISION in the U.S.

"A look at the beginning of Community Television Broadcasting and its future"

DR. SYLVESTER CARAWAY JR.

WRITERS REPUBLIC L.L.C.
515 Summit Ave. Unit R1
Union City, NJ 07087, USA

Website: *www.writersrepublic.com*
Hotline: *1-877-656-6838*
Email: *info@writersrepublic.com*

Ordering Information:
Quantity sales. Special discounts are available on quantity purchases by corporations, associations, and others. For details, contact the publisher at the address above.

Library of Congress Control Number: 2021908093
ISBN-13:   978-1-63728-487-2   [Paperback Edition]
                  978-1-63728-488-9   [Hardback Edition]
                  978-1-63728-489-6   [Digital Edition]

Rev. date: 04/15/2021

This book is dedicated to those who are thinking in the television broadcasting anywhere around the world. If you ever been in your local community broadcast station. You've reach your first step to moving on to either Public TV, cable television networks or mainstream broadcast networks, Again, anywhere around the world.

TABLE OF CONTENTS

BIOGRAPHY

Dr. Sylvester Caraway Jr. Was born in Los Angeles, California, but grew up in the city of Compton, California, which a section of Compton turned to the new city of Carson in the mid-70s. Attended Ralph Bunch Elementary school and Enterprise Junior High school and 1 year at Compton High school. After a violent occurrence happened at Compton High school, our parents put us in Gardena High school (myself and my 2 bothers). After graduating from Gardena High School in 1974, he and 6 of his school buddies all joined the Air Force. Sylvester served 20 years, 4 months and 12 days on active duty in the United States Air Force from 1974 to 1994 as a combat cameraman. As a warrior, himself, he first served as an administration clerk for 3 years and then transferred to become a combat cameraman on flying status for the rest of my career. We also had a family band, called "*The Caraway Four*". We competed against "The Jackson Five", "The Silvers" and other youth bands during the early 50's, 60's and early 70's. We did cut one album which the songs were written by our last manager Lester Bowie who used to play guitar with James Brown. I later played while in the Air Force with other soldiers in local clubs and NCO's and Officer's clubs on several bases it was stationed.

The reason for this change in my career, I felt I was not accomplishing what I originally set out to do in the Air Force. That was to do something substantial or more meaningful in my career to defend the United States and its citizens. I have traveled to several countries documenting and recording the good, bad and the ugly at times in wars, military training exercises, and a few conflicts around the world. I genuinely enjoyed my life as an administration clerk, because I was assigned to the 773 Tactical Airlift Squadron (C-130 cargo plane) at Dyess Air Force base, in Abilene, Texas. Here I traveled to the United Kingdom, Germany and Panama while working in the post office and administration, or what was called the "orderly room" for the 300 other Dyess Air Force base troops that were deployed to these countries that we supported.

However, I genuinely enjoyed being a combat cameraman where I traveled the world to places, I would never have the chance to do on my own. Like the Far East, Spain, Cuba, Norway, Greenland, Iceland, Central and South America, Africa, Europe, United Kingdom, Japan, South Korea and Turkey. Well, enough of my military career. Though, after I did retire from the United States Air Force, I was already enrolled at Sacramento City College and then moved on to California State University, Sacramento and accomplished my masters, masters with honors and PhD in Philosophy at Griffith University, Nathan campus, Queensland, Australia for 9 years with a minor in TV broadcasting.

Now he is an accomplished author of 2 music scores registered with the Library of Congress. He also has written 3 University studies. Along as also an established book author. One book is called *"From Slavery to Fighting for Recognition"*. He also working on another book: *"The Relationship Between the Native Americans and the African Americans"*. Worked as a floor manager for Paramount's most popular TV morning show series *"Good Day Sacramento"* which was rated number 2 next to *"Good Morning America"*. Worked as an Assistant Director for ABC's Special TV snow series Eye on LA with the host Chuck Henry *"The Ghost on the Queen Mary"* ship in Long Beach, California. Worked as Producer and Director for the California State Fair on their video production of top musical and up a coming up musical talent. Worked as a Producer for both San Bernardino and Sacramento's community broadcasting stations. Also work as Executive Producer for Brisbane's community station in Queensland, Australia. He also works at the Korean TV broadcast network in South Korea as the night shift Producer and Master Control at nights. This TV station was called Armed Forces Korean Network (AFKN). Now, he just writes about different topics that he finds of interest to the world. Dr. Sylvester "Sly" Caraway Jr. the future will also become the Executive Director and President of MCCHSM Board of the Directors of the US Military Combat Camera History and Stories Museum: www.mcchsm.org

INTRODUCTION

Public, Educational, and Government Access

Public access television began in North America in the late 1960s and early 1970s as a radical experiment in democratic communication. Access television supporters hoped to break the lock which commercial interests held on the television medium by bringing non-profit, grassroots political and cultural programming directly to people's living rooms. By securing inexpensive access to production resources and facilities, such as cameras, microphones, studios, and editing equipment, ordinary citizens would be able to construct their own televisual messages and to bypass the framing devices of professional, corporate media.1 Distribution would be accomplished by cablecasting programs on a first-come, first-served basis over local cable systems. Supporters envisioned access television as a public space where, liberated from the economic and editorial constraints of commercial television production, citizens could air their views over the most powerful and pervasive communications medium of the era. With twenty-five years of access television practice behind us and calls for access to yet another new technology -- the computer network -- before us, the question should be asked: Is access television an effective tool for democratic communication? One way to gauge the democratic potential of access television is to examine the strategic use of this resource by radical media projects.

Following Downing's (1984, p. 2) definition, the term radical media here applies to media which pose challenges to existing power structures, empower diverse communities and classes, and enable communities of interest to speak to each other. These kinds of media are seldom distributed by American commercial or public television, and their experiences are indicative of the possibilities and limits of access television as a democratic medium. This study profiles three projects Access Television & Political Communication 3 currently utilizing access television as a tool for progressive political communication. Drawing on theories of democracy and democratic communication, the study analyzes both the political achievements of these projects and the structural limitations of access television as a forum for democratic communication. The study concludes that while public access has opened a space for grassroots political communication on television, a restructuring of access television resources would further strengthen the democratic potential of the medium. To begin, I will briefly review the set of circumstances in which access television came into being and its current structure. The same political and economic factors which precipitated the development of access television also have limited the nature of the services it provides.

Access television represents a unique moment in the history of technology in the U.S. where progressive groups have managed to secure a genuine public space in the electronic media. Yet, this space has been underutilized by these groups, subject to inadequate funding, and devoid of government and industry support. A Brief History of Public Access Television In the early 1970s, broadcast television consisted of three network channels and a fledgling public broadcasting system. Cable technology seemed to offer a genuine alternative to this highly centralized, broadcast market. Although cable had been developed in the 1940s, it was only in the 1970s that it metamorphosed from a technology for extending broadcast reception into a technology able to originate programming over its systems. With its new-found ability for program origination, its 12-channel carrying capacity, and its image as a local provider of services to discrete communities, cable inspired visions of a more diverse, decentralized, and competitive television market. As one early commentator enthused, "Television can become far more flexible, far more democratic, far more diversified in content, and for more responsive to the full range of pressing needs in today's cities, neighborhoods, towns, and Access Television & Political Communication 4 communities" (Smith, 1970, p. 8). The democratic promise of cable was espoused by cable operators, economists of regulation, liberals, policy makers, and progressive groups (Streeter, 1987, p. 181).

Access television came about in large part through a temporary confluence of interests among cable operators, federal regulators, and access activists. Access activism in the 1970s was an outgrowth of 1960s social activism which advocated participatory democracy as a means to social and cultural change. The alternative print media of the 1960s sought to create an alternative consciousness in their readers and, ultimately, an alternative culture (Armstrong, 1981, pp. 20-24). Access activism extended the goals of the 1960s radical press to the medium of television. Access activists hoped community members would be able to utilize cable systems, along with consumer video equipment, to engage in unmediated expression, to increase communication between and among themselves, and to discover and define a grassroots political agenda.2 Michael Shamberg, author of Guerrilla Media, which became known as the "Bible" of alternative media, praised cable's potential to create an alternative information infrastructure, or a "grassroots network of indigenous media activity" (Shamberg, 1971, p. 9). Though inspired by technological developments, access activists also saw the need to realize their goals in concrete communications policy. The Alternate Media Center in New York, founded by documentarists George Stoney and Red Burns, served as the organizational center for the political instigation and popularization of access television in the U.S. (Hénaut, 1991, p. 96; Engelman, 1990, pp. 18-20). Federal regulators and cable operators were also instrumental in establishing access television.

The Federal Communication Commission (FCC) saw an opportunity to promote local programming policies in cable where they had failed with broadcast television. In 1972 the FCC mandated that larger cable operators provide public, educational and governmental (PEG) access channels, equipment, and facilities (Cable Television Report and Order, 1972) to the communities they served. Cable operators had Access Television & Political Communication 5 their own reasons to support the local and community programming potential of cable. Volunteering to provide PEG channels was one way to curry favor with the FCC, which had halted cable expansion from 1968 to 1972 while it deliberated over rules for the medium, and perhaps to preempt federally mandated access television requirements. The offer of PEG channels and services to local communities was also good public relations for cable companies competing among themselves to secure a municipal cable franchise. Early government and industry support led many communities to believe they could rely on the good will of cable operators to supply access television resources and facilities, to adequately fund access television operations, and in some cases to manage public access channels and facilities. (Laura Stein, Ph.D., 2001)

CHAPTER 1

The Beginning of Television in United States

In short, it is important to highlight the beginning of television broadcasting launched on 7 September 1927 in the United States and why in the future was the reason why community television broadcast services were important to the average citizen. Since the invention of broadcasting television over the airwaves of television began, there were only three networks American Broadcast Corporation (ABC), Columbia Broadcast Service (CBS) and National Broadcast Corporation (NBC). It is also important address other countries broadcast television services.

ABC: The American Broadcasting Corporation (ABC) is an American commercial broadcast television network that is a flagship property of Disney–ABC Television Group, a subsidiary of the Disney Media Networks division of The Walt Disney Company. The network is headquartered on Columbus Avenue and West 66th Street in Manhattan, New York City. There are additional major offices and production facilities elsewhere in New York City, as well as in Los Angeles and Burbank, California.

CBS: CBS (an initialism of the network›s former name, the Columbia Broadcasting System) is an American English language commercial broadcast television and radio network that is a flagship property of CBS Corporation. The company is headquartered at the CBS Building in New York City with major production facilities and operations in

New York City (at the CBS Broadcast Center) and Los Angeles (at CBS Television City and the CBS Studio Center).

NBC: The National Broadcasting Corporation (NBC) is an American English language commercial broadcast television network that is a flagship property of NBC Universal, a subsidiary of Comcast. The network is headquartered at 30 Rockefeller Plaza in New York City, with additional major offices near Los Angeles (at 10 Universal City Plaza), Chicago (at the NBC Tower) and Philadelphia (at the Comcast Technology Center). The network is one of the Big Three television networks. NBC is sometimes referred to as the "Peacock Network", about its stylized peacock logo, introduced in 1956 to promote the company's innovations in early color broadcasting. It became the network's official emblem in 1979.

No one knew that these three major television broadcasters were going to grow to be conglomerates later. But, having just these three major networks community television wasn't a thought of until later in the early 1960's. Community broadcast television consideration was due the expansion and the coming of cable and satellite services that the Federal Communications Commission (FCC) ruled that the airwaves belong to the public and when cable companies sprouted up, such as Time Warner, COMCAST, DIRECT TV, DISH etc. the FCC ruled that these cable companies had to provide television access to the local communities that they were serving. That way the public could make their own television programs, which later came the public, educational and local government television channels. Known as public, educational and government (PEG's).

The first television, an electromechanical device capable of producing exceedingly small and blurry monochrome images, was developed in 1884. The first transmission of images using this device occurred in 1925. Philo Farnsworth developed the first electronic television in 1927, and the first TV station. This experiment is believed to be the first demonstration of a working electro-mechanical television system. 1972: According to the Grolier Encyclopedia, the electronic television was successfully displayed for the first time on Sept. 7, 1927 in San

Francisco. This predecessor of the modern television was invented by Philo Taylor Farnsworth, a 21-year-old Utah native.

The 1950s was a time of remarkable achievement in television, but this was not the case for the entire medium. American viewers old enough to remember TV in the '50s may fondly recall the shows of Sid Caesar, Jackie Gleason, Milton Berle, and Lucille Ball, but such high-quality programs were the exception; most of television during its formative years could be aptly described, as it was by one Broadway playwright, as "amateurs playing at home movies." The underlying problem was not a shortage of talented writers, producers, and performers; there were plenty, but they were already busily involved on the Broadway stage and in vaudeville, radio, and motion pictures. Consequently, television drew chiefly on a talent pool of individuals who had not achieved success in the more popular media and on the young and inexperienced who were years from reaching their potential. Nevertheless, the new medium ultimately proved so fascinating a technical novelty that in the early stages of its development the quality of its content seemed almost not to matter. Then became another source of television watching that was funded by public dollars, Public Broadcasting Service (PBS), which is headed by the for Corporation Public Broadcasting (CPB) The Corporation for Public Broadcasting is an American non-profit corporation created in 1967 by an act of the United States Congress and funded by the American people, as stated under their logo in use since 2000, to promote and help support public broadcasting.

PBS is an American public broadcaster and television program distributor. It is a nonprofit organization and the most prominent provider of educational television programming to public television stations in the United States, distributing series such as American Experience, America's Test Kitchen, Antiques Roadshow, Arthur, Barney & Friends, Clifford the Big Red Dog, Downton Abbey, Finding Your Roots, Frontline, The Magic School Bus, Masterpiece, Mister Rogers' Neighborhood, Nature, Nova, the PBS NewsHour, Reading Rainbow, Sesame Street, Teletubbies, and This Old House.

PBS is funded by a combination of member station dues, the Corporation for Public Broadcasting, National Data cast, pledge drives, and donations from both private foundations and individual citizens.

All proposed funding for programming is subject to a set of standards to ensure the program is free of influence from the funding source. Since the mid-2000s, Roper Opinion Research polls commissioned by PBS have consistently placed the service as the *most-trusted national institution* in the United States. A 2016–2017 study by Nielsen Media Research found 80% of all US television households view the network's programs over the course of a year. However, PBS is not responsible for all programming carried on public television stations, a large proportion of which may come from its member stations, including WGBH-TV, WETA-TV, WNET, WTTW, WHYY-TV, Twin Cities PBS, American Public Television, and independent producers. This distinction regarding the origin of different programs on the service present a frequent source of viewer confusion. PBS was established on November 3, 1969 by Hartford N. Gunn Jr. (president of WGBH), John Macy (president of CPB), James Day (last president of National Educational Television), and Kenneth A. Christiansen (chairman of the department of broadcasting at the University of Florida), PBS began operations on October 5, 1970, taking over many of the functions of its predecessor, National Educational Television (NET), which later merged with Newark, New Jersey station WNDT to form WNET. In 1973, it merged with Educational Television Stations.

Immediately after public disclosure of the Watergate scandal, on May 17, 1973, the United States Senate Watergate Committee commenced proceedings; PBS broadcast the proceedings nationwide, with Robert MacNeil and Jim Lehrer as commentators. For seven months, nightly "gavel-to-gavel" broadcasts drew great public interest, and raised the profile of the fledgling PBS network

The History of Community or Public Access TV and PEG TV Industries

Public-access television was created in the United States between 1969 by the Federal Communications Commission (FCC), under Chairman Dean Burch, based on pioneering work and advocacy of George Stoney, Red Burns (Alternate Media Center), and Sidney Dean (City Club of NY) which provided airways for public citizens to show their creativity. Public-access television is a sometimes-bizarre world where anyone with the time and inclination can appear on television. It is where you find the rants of Columbus, Ohio, goth Damon Zex and the strange instructional videos of Let's Paint TV, where Los Angeles host John Kilduff taught viewers how to paint and make blended drinks all while exercising on a treadmill. Then there is my personal favorite What's Your Problem? the story of a man having a hard time eating a fish. Public, Education and Government (PEG) television was introduced in the media landscape. Having the national advocacy group Alternate Media Center changed in mid-70's local groups took over the licensing and management of all national community television broadcast stations. There are hundreds of Community Television (CTV) stations nationwide and since I live in Greensboro, North Carolina, I will focus on this station in this chapter. Greensboro Community Television, Inc. is a not-for-profit 501 (c)(3) corporation created to operate and manage the public access channel as provided for in the North Carolina Cable Franchise Act. The funding source for Greensboro Community Television is that it receives a portion of the taxes that are collected from the publics cable bill. This money is collected by the state of NC, and an exceedingly small percentage is then distributed to the public access facilities in the state. This pays for about half of their operations budget. The rest of their funding comes from user fees, video production, grants, and other forms of fundraising. They usually have quite a shortfall in their budget. The Greensboro's community television broadcasts over cable services and not free-to-air and charges $100.00 for an orientation fee.

Public-access television came about with the rise of cable television in the late '70s and early '80s. In exchange for the rights to lay cable wires on public land, cable companies were required to donate a portion of their revenue to provide facilities and airtime to allow public comment. (Such agreements are negotiated on a city-by-city basis). The idea was to give voice to ordinary citizens who otherwise would not have access to any media outlets. In 1984, the Cable Franchise Policy and Communications Act prohibited cable operators from exercising any editorial control over public-access channels. Thus public-access TV mostly became famous for its eccentric personalities and bizarre shows. (A few break-out stars even got their start on public access, like comedian Tom Green and horror hostess Elvira.) But it has also been a venue for serious political and philosophical discussion, a place to find the recorded minutes of your local town hall meeting or school board discussion, as well as a springboard for citizen journalism. In the 1990s, Lisa Hendrick videotaped city council meetings in Marine City, Mich., to expose inappropriate behavior by elected officials. And many public-access stations rebroadcast investigative pieces by Democracy Now, Free Speech TV and Deep-Dish TV Network

However, most of the community television stations are labeled CTV stations and most are not on free-to-air. For example, at the Greensboro, North Carolina's local community broadcast station, they are on cable television and not on free-to-air. They call this station Public Access Television, which not to confuse it with Public Broadcast Services (PBS). This community broadcast station charges a one-time fee of $100.00 fee allows a producer to submit programs to be cablecast 8 on Greensboro Community Television. This CTV station also gives the member eligibility for a series contract, as well as the option of class enrollment and equipment use once certified on the equipment. Class fees are not included in the membership fee. Below is the North Carolina Cable Franchise Act. If you are already working in a CTV station or just doing research. Other Cable Franchise Acts might be different then North Carolina. However, most local CTV stations normally charge $25.00 and some even allow to use the video equipment away from the station. It varies by city-to-city.

Public, Educational and Government Channels (PEG)

Initially, there were three major television networks know as the 1st tier sector ABC, CBS and NBC. The 2nd tier sector is PBS, Educational and Government television broadcasters. The 3rd tier sector public or (community) television broadcasters. This is the Public, Educational and Government (PEG Channels.) A city with a population of at least 50,000 is allowed a minimum of three initial PEG channels plus any channels more than this minimum that are activated, as of July 1, 2006, under the terms of an existing franchise agreement whose franchise area includes the city. A city with a population of less than 50,000 is allowed a minimum of two initial PEG channels plus any channels more than this minimum that are activated, as of July 1, 2006, under the terms of an existing franchise agreement whose franchise area includes the city. For a city included in the franchise area of an existing agreement, the agreement determines the service tier placement and transmission quality of the initial PEG channels. For a city that is not included in the franchise area of an existing agreement, the initial PEG channels must be on a basic service tier, and the transmission quality of the channels must be equivalent to those of the closest city covered by an existing agreement.

A county is allowed a minimum of two initial PEG channels plus any channels more than this minimum that are activated, as of July 1, 2006, under the terms of an existing franchise agreement whose franchise area includes the county. For a county included in the franchise area of an existing agreement, the agreement determines the service tier placement and transmission quality of the initial PEG channels. For a county that is not included in the franchise area of an existing agreement, the initial PEG channels must be on a basic service tier and the transmission quality of the channels must be equivalent to those of any city with PEG channels in the county. The cable service provider must maintain the same channel designation for a PEG channel unless the service area of the State-issued franchise includes PEG channels that are operated by different counties or cities and those PEG channels have the same channel designation. Each county and city whose PEG channels are served by the same cable system headend must cooperate with each other and with the cable system provider in sharing the capacity needed to provide the PEG channels. Additional PEG Channels. - A county or city that does not have seven PEG channels, including the initial PEG channels, is eligible for an additional PEG channel if it meets the programming requirements in this subsection. A county or city that has seven PEG channels is not eligible for an additional channel.

A county or city that meets the programming requirements in this subsection may make a written request under subsection (b) of this section for an additional channel. The additional channel may be provided on any service tier. The transmission quality of the additional channel must be at least equivalent to the transmission quality of the other channels provided. The PEG channels operated by a county or city must meet the following programming requirements for at least 120 continuous days for the county or city to obtain an additional channel:

> (1) All of the PEG channels must have scheduled programming for at least eight hours a day.

> (2) The programming content of each of the PEG channels must not repeat more than fifteen percent (15%) of the programming content on any of the other PEG channels.

> (3) No more than fifteen percent (15%) of the programming content on any of the PEG channels may be character-generated programming.

(e) Use of Channels. – If a county or city no longer provides any programming for transmission over a PEG channel it has activated, the channel may be reprogrammed at the cable service provider's discretion. A cable service provider must give at least a 60-day notice to a county or city before it reprograms a PEG channel that is not used. The cable service provider must restore a previously lost PEG channel within 120 days of the date a county or city certifies to the provider a schedule that demonstrates the channel will be used.

(f) Operation of Channels. – A cable service provider is responsible only for the transmission of a PEG channel. The county or city to which the PEG channel is provided is responsible for the operation and content of the channel. A county or city that provides content to a cable service provider for transmission on a PEG channel is considered to have authorized the provider to transmit the content throughout the provider's service area, regardless of whether part of the service area is outside the boundaries of the county or city.

All programming on a PEG channel must be noncommercial. A cable service provider may not brand content on a PEG channel with its logo, name, or other identifying marks.

A cable service provider is not required to transmit content on a PEG channel that is branded with the logo, name, or other identifying marks of another cable service provider.

(g) Compliance. - A county or city that has not received PEG channel capacity as required by this section may bring an action to compel a cable service provider to comply with this section.

§ 66-358. Transmission of PEG channels.

(a) Service. - A cable service provider operating under a State-issued franchise must transmit a PEG channel by one of the following methods:

(1) Interconnection with another cable system operated in its service area. A cable service provider operating in the same service area as a provider under a State-issued franchise must interconnect its cable system on reasonable and competitively neutral terms with the other provider's cable system within 120 days after it receives a written request for interconnection and may not refuse to interconnect on these terms. The terms include compensation for costs incurred in interconnecting. Interconnection may be accomplished by direct cable, microwave link, satellite, or another method of connection.

(2) Transmission of the signal from each PEG channel programmer's origination site if the origination site is in the provider's service area.

(b) Signal. - All PEG channel programming provided to a cable service provider for transmission must meet the federal National Television System Committee standards or the Advanced Television Systems Committee Standards. If a PEG channel programmer complies with these standards and the cable service provider cannot transmit the programming without altering the transmission signal, then the cable service provider must do one of the following:

(1) Alter the transmission signal to make it compatible with the technology or protocol the cable service provider uses to deliver its cable service.

(2) Provide to the county or city the equipment needed to alter the transmission signal to make it compatible with the technology or protocol the cable service provider uses to deliver its cable service.

66-359. PEG Cannel Grants.

(a) PEG Channel Fund. - The PEG Channel Fund is created as an interest-bearing special revenue fund. It consists of revenue allocated to it under G.S. 105-164.44I(b) and any other revenues appropriated to it. The e-NC Authority, created under G.S. 143B-437.46, administers the Fund.

(b) Grants. - A county or city may apply to the e-NC Authority for a grant from the PEG Channel Fund. In awarding grants from the Fund, the e-NC Authority must, to the extent possible, select applicants from all parts of the State based upon need. Grants from the Fund are subject to the following limitations:

(1) The grant may not exceed twenty-five thousand dollars ($25,000).

(2) The applicant must match the grant on a dollar-for-dollar basis.

(3) The grant may be used only for capital expenditures necessary to provide PEG channel programming.

(4) An applicant may receive no more than one grant per fiscal year.

According to the FCC and in the one example, the North Carolina Cable Franchise Act is a community television that has been formed for mass media in which a television station is owned, operated or programmed by a community group to provide television programs of local interest known as local programming. Community television stations are most operated by non-profit groups or cooperatives. However, in some cases they may be operated by a local college or university, a cable company, or a municipal government. Public, educational and government access television is a form of non-commercial mass media where ordinary people can create content which can be viewed through cable TV systems. Standard public-access television is often grouped with Educational-access television and Government-access television (GATV) channels, by the acronym PEG. PEG Channels are typically only available on cable television systems.

According to W.D. Sherman (Bill) Olson, in his book "This History of Public Television". Mass media have never guaranteed access by the common man. Throughout history, each new medium seemed to tip the balance of equal expression further in favor of the wealthy elite. Literacy gave the written word to those who could afford an education. Newspapers, magazines, radio, and television have had exclusive ownership, and paid advertising as a means of personal expression has been hindered by high rates. Even the notion of publicly owned airwaves has never guaranteed people automatic access to them. The common man's traditional forum has often been a soapbox in the town-square - a strong voice on a busy street corner.

The FCC Cable Communications Act of 1984 Section 622

In the United States, public access television is an alternative system of television which originated as a response to disenchantment with the commercial broadcasting system, and order to fulfill some of the social potential of cable television. In the United States, every community that is served by one or more cable TV companies has the right to collect a cable television franchise fee, based on the FCC's Cable Communications Act of 1984 Section 622, from those cable companies to fund a Public-access television cable TV channel. Public access television is one of the most exciting and controversial U.S. media developments within the past two decades.

When cable television began to be widely introduced in the early 1970s, the Federal Communications Commission (FCC) mandated in 1972 that "beginning in 1972, new cable systems [and after 1977, all cable systems] in the 100 largest television markets be required to provide channels for government, for educational purpose, and most importantly, for public access" This mandate suggested that cable systems should make available three public access channels to be used for state and local government, education, and community public access use.

"Public Access" (PBS) was construed to mean that the cable company should make available equipment and airtime so that literally anybody could make noncommercial use of the access channel and say and do anything they wished on a first-come, first-served basis. Subject only to obscenely and libel laws. The result was an entirely different sort of programming, reflecting the interest of groups and individuals usually excluded from mainstream television. Beginning in the 1970s, cable systems began to offer access channels to the public. So that groups and individuals could make programs for other individuals in their own communities. Access systems began to proliferate, and access programming is now being cablecast regularly in such places as New York, Los Angeles, Boston, Chicago, Atlanta, Madison, Urbana, Austin, and per hour American Public TV Stations (APTS) as many as 1,200 other towns or regions.

America's Public Television Stations (APTS) is a nonprofit membership organization ensuring a strong and financially sound public television system and helping member stations provide essential public services in education, public safety, and civic leadership to the American people. This organization serves all the PBS stations nationwide. Its affiliate APTS Action, Inc. promotes the legislative and regulatory interests of noncommercial television stations at the national level through direct advocacy and through grass tops and grassroots campaigns designed to garner bipartisan political support. The public television system is comprised of 170 licensees operating more than 350 public television stations across America and serving more than 98 percent of the American people. About half of these licensees are nonprofit community foundations. The rest are State, university and local school district licensees. All are locally owned, locally operated, and locally oriented in their programming and community services, and all share a mission of serving everyone, everywhere, every day for free – including in places where no model for commercial success exists. Here is where you can go too to see how many public access stations (PBS) there are in the United States: https://apts.org/about/membership.

Today, in the 21st Century, this cornerstone of giving speeches in the public square was once swarming with pedestrians is dying and replaced by shopping malls whose corporate owners prohibit protesters and orators. But in many communities with cable television, the common man has a new soapbox - one from which his voice can potentially reach thousands of cable subscribers. There are three tiers to the television industry. Tier one is the major television networks to include satellite and cable stations. Public access TV (PBS) is in the second tier of television broadcaster. These others are in the third-tier sector of television broadcast, also called cable access, community access, community television, and PEG (Public, Education and Government). In the third-tier sector, these stations provide television production equipment, training, and airtime on a local cable channel, so members of the public can produce their own shows and televise them to a mass audience. In the United States, public access depends on the cable medium. Community Antenna Television began in Astoria, Oregon, when L. E. Parsons erected an antenna atop the hotel in which he lived to receive the broadcasts of KRSC-TV in Seattle, Washington.

Called Community Television, or Public Access, Educational, and Governmental Access in the United States. Community television represents our single source for media access in the United States public. Also, with the introduction of the Internet, a few PEG's can now spread their messages internationally. With more than 2,000 community groups providing some 15,000 hours of original programming each week—more than the annual output of ABC, CBS, and NBC combined—Community Television compares broadcasting and grassroots cablecasting in the form of public, educational, and government (PEG) access.

The ideal was to create an access system required, in many cases, setting up a local organization to manage the access channels, though in other systems the cable company itself managed the access center.

In the beginning, however, few, if any cable systems made as many as three channels available, but some systems began offering one or two access channels in the early to mid-1970s. The availability of access channels depended, for the most part, on the political clout of local governments and committed, and often unpaid, local groups to convince the cable companies, almost all privately owned, to make available an access channel. A 1979 Supreme Court decision, however, struck down the 1972 FCC ruling on the grounds that the FCC had no authority to mandate access, an authority which supposedly belongs to the U.S. Congress alone. Nonetheless, cable was expanding so rapidly and becoming such a high-growth competitive industry that by the 1980s city governments considering cable systems were besieged by companies making lucrative offers (20 to 80 channel cable systems) and were able to demand access channels and financial support for public access systems as part of their contract negotiations. Consequently, public access grew significantly during the 1980s and 1990s.

Not surprisingly, public access television has been controversial from the beginning. Early disputes revolved around explicit sexuality and obscenity, in New York city public access schedules with programs like "Ugly George' and "Midnight Blue" drawing attention. Focus then turned to controversial political content when extremist groups such as the Ku Klux Klan and the Aryan Nation began distributing programs nationally. Many groups like the American Atheists, labor groups, and a diverse number of political groups began producing programs for syndication, and debates emerged over whether access systems should show programming that was not actually produced in the community where it was originally cable casted from.

Despite the controversy, public access television is currently thriving. A very few systems charge money for use of facilities or charge a fee for use of air time, but due to competitive bidding among cable systems in the 1980s and 1990s for the most lucrative franchises, many cable systems offer free use of equipment, personnel, and air time, and occasionally even provide free videotapes. In these situations, literally anyone can make use of public access facilities without technical expertise, television experience, or financial resources. Many public access systems also offer a range of conceptual and technical training programs designed to instruct groups or individuals who wish to make their own programs from conception through final editing. As video equipment costs have rapidly declined it has even become possible for some groups to purchase their own equipment. In the 1990s, following the trends of talk radio, many talk television access shows emerged. Individuals fielded calls from members of the community, and discussed current political problems, or, in some cases, personal problems. In many ways, this "conversational" mode exemplifies the community focus and personal orientation of access television, again moving away from mainstream TV designed to reach the largest possible audiences.

But various actions moving toward greater media deregulation in the 1990s threaten the continued survival of access, as do the Internet and other new communications technologies. In highly competitive environment, cable systems may very well close-down access systems if there is insufficient government pressure to keep them open, thought completive market pressures might promote the survival of popular access channels. And, while the Internet, and other emerging delivery systems could render obsolete the relatively low-tech access systems, these same forms of communication may even multiply access television, enabling literally any group or individual to make their television programs and distribute them over the Internet. Thus, the future of access in uncertain and is bound up with the unforeseeable consequences of what may be one of the most dramatic communications revolutions in history.

As community television was supposed to be for local groups to form management for each community broadcast station. As well, community television was formed to allow individual's a chance to be part of the television broadcast industry. Although, this was mainly formed widespread for the interest of local groups and individuals. However, there was no advocate association that was formed to lobby its interest to the U.S. Congress, until 1979. In 1979, the Association for Public Television Stations rose to be the main advocacy reprehensive of community, public and PEG's nationwide.

Since living in Greensboro, North Carolina from 2010 to 2022, here is an example of the community broadcast station in Greensboro, North Carolina offers. Greensboro Community Television (Cable 8) provides

Greensboro-area residents, organizations, agencies and institutions with television program time, training, equipment, production, and related services on a first-come, first-served non-discriminatory basis, free from censorship. The primary goal of Greensboro Community Television is to promote free expression of diverse ideas and facilitate first amendment rights of free speech on the designated access channels by coordinating the use of the channels and providing cablecast facilities, technical assistance and training to any individual, group or organization interested in producing educational, cultural, informational or other community-oriented television programs. Greensboro Community Television, Inc. is a not-for-profit 501c3 corporation created to operate and manage the public access channel as provided for in the North Carolina Cable Franchise Act. However, their channel is not on free-to-air, i.e., they are on a cable system.

The North Carolina Cable Franchise Act Applies to existing 7% state sales tax to all video programming services (i.e., satellites are included.) Low Frequency Active (LFA) to receive an approximation of fees they would have received. Establishes annual $25K capital grant for equipment on dollar-for-dollar match (capped at $2M PEG per year) LFA can recover from all providers separate PEG fee in place at time of enactment. In this example of this community television broadcaster. Its primary goal of Greensboro Community Television is to promote free expression of diverse ideas and facilitate first amendment rights of free speech on the designated access channels by coordinating the use of the channels and providing cablecast facilities, technical assistance and training to any individual, group or organization interested in producing educational, cultural, informational or other community-oriented television programs.

Although, the Greensboro's Community Broadcast Television station (CTV) does allow access free access to its services. To become a member with this community television station, will costs a one-time fee of $100.00 just for the initial orientation. Greensboro Community Television plays what we receive. Any citizen of Guilford County, NC can submit a program for cablecast once they have paid their yearly membership fee. The majority of what you see on Channel 8 has been produced by a community member just like yourself! So, if you see a program on Cable 8, someone who lives in Greensboro or Guilford County has requested that it be shown. It does offer free training of the equipment and its bylaws. The CTV station only receives a portion of the taxes that are collected from the public's cable bill, plus special class lesson fees. This money is collected by the state of NC, and an exceedingly small percentage is then distributed to the public access facilities in the state. This pays for about half of our operations budget. The rest of our funding comes from user fees, video production, grants and other forms of fundraising.

They usually have quite a shortfall in their budget. Any contributions are always greatly appreciated and are most always tax deductible. However, this community television station only airs on cable services and not free-to-air antennas. There are also other local community television broadcasters only offering cable TV services and not on free-to-air antennas, where it should have either both or just free-to-air only, since its supported by and 75% of this station's revenue coming from members fees and city taxes. This forces the local public to subscribe to their local cable services necessary to have access to channel 8 in Greensboro, North Carolina.

Who Runs Public (Community) Access TV Channels?

It is supposed and meant for the public to own, manage and operate the television station if licensed by the Federal Communications Committee (FCC). In one case where Dr. Caraway's Ph.D. research on Australian community television industry, he found that only one (Brisbane) community television (CTV) stations of the four was owned by the public with their board of directors, and the local public managed and operated the station. The other two were operated on university campuses (Sydney and Melbourne), and the last one (Adelaide) was operating more as a private company. Though within public use, the operators were not including much of the public but producing their own internal productions. Public access television may give you a visions of the movie comedy "Wayne's World" parodies, but for many people around the United States, public access TV or community access television is a vital way to share information, creativity and foster community relations. These community television broadcast stations maybe used for the public, education, or local/state government; called PEGs. There are over 5000 PEGs nationwide in the United States and 100's more around the world.

By its very definition, public access television is a free channel that airs programming created by the members of the public. The advent of public access TV occurred in the early 1970s under Section 611 of the Communications Act, a landmark decision that gave local franchising authorities the ability to require cable companies to set aside channels for public, educational or governmental (PEG) use. A franchising authority is, in most cases, a city or municipality that has a contract with a cable company that defines the services that will be provided to the community. Local franchising authorities are not mandated by federal law to request the channels, it is an option they can exercise at will.

Public access channels also are known as community access, community television or cable access channels. A public access channel can be run by a cable company or by a third party designated by the cable company. Regardless of which party operates the channel, it must offer the crucial gear and knowledge that goes along with producing television, too. This includes making the studio, equipment, and behind-the-scenes staff available to people who want to air a show on public access television. Most guidelines also include free training on specialized tracks (some CTV stations charge for specialized classes), from on-air to production. Public access television is available in communities across the United States, and Canada, and in countries such as the United Kingdom, Australia, New Zealand, South Africa, Austria, Fiji and more.

Public access television broadcasters may vary by region, and in most cases, to become a member or being able to broadcast any media the individual or group would need to attend an orientation and take production training classes before airing your own program on cable access TV. Although it may seem like a completely altruistic move to allow the public to freely create TV shows for the broader community, it is not entirely without cost. In fact, if you are a cable subscriber, you are probably paying for the shows that air on public access TV. The fee that shows up on your cable bill depends on the percentage of revenues a municipality has asked a cable company to pay and the cable tier you have purchased. In this case of the public's cable bill has a percentage going towards paying for your local community station. It makes since that in the case of Greensboro's community television station should not just be cable. It should also offer a free-to-air channel as well for those who are not forced to have their TV watching taxed.

In the United States and most every other country that has community television broadcasting stations the management of the station reflects more to the third-tier sector and with the interest of the local community, i.e., General Managers. However, when Dr. Caraway was in Australia from 2001 to 2009 and worked as the Executive Producer of the Brisbane's CTV station in the state of Queensland. We had a General Manager then me and producers and other staff below them. Dr. Caraway's PhD was about the Australia's community television industry, titled *"The Development of Commercialism"*. He was even the first to ever write about this industry when they began in the 1970s. Later, in 2009, there was radical change their management titles from General Manager to Chief Executive Officer. Even, their broadcasting made them seem more commercialized than being more local. They were broadcasting older cartoons and sitcoms from the United States and other English-speaking countries. Even their programming, which dominated most of their airtime was more in line with commercial television broadcasters rather then most CTV stations worldwide. Since 2009, the Australian community broadcast stations heads now call themselves Chief Executive Officers (CEOs). Two of their CTV stations are on university campus (Sydney and Melbourne) and two others (Brisbane and Adelaide) are within the public areas which allows their local community to get involved.

In conclusion in this chapter, I had to bring this matter up with what was going on in Australia. Can the management titles of other CTV stations worldwide also change from General Manager to CEO's? To my understanding of and it most cases the public's view of CTV station is perceived to be public when the management title is General Manager and not CEO. This CEO image I believe will harm the image of Australia's CTV stations with their public and their federal government on how they are perceived as functioning more to corporation style entities rather than a third-tier level non-profit media that they are licensed.

The future of Community Broadcasting: Civil Society and Communications Policy

Will community television one day be lamented in the same way as the Glenn Valley Bridge Club in Pennsylvania, where no one remains 'who can tell us precisely when or why the group broke up' (Putnam, 2000: 15)? Robert Putnam's bestseller Bowling Alone proposed that people 'need to reconnect with one another' and rebuild their communities for the good of society. Although he may not have succeeded in instigating a revival of lawn bowls and bridge, Putnam did spark a debate about the meaning of "community" today and its role in bringing about positive social change. At a time when the communications landscape is set to transform with the introduction of digital broadcasting technology, this thesis looks at the status of community broadcasting and its role within civil society. Taking Australia's community television sector as its starting point, it aims to define the pressures, public philosophies and policy decisions that make community broadcasting what it is. This thesis is structured thematically and geographically. The introductory chapters establish the research question in relation to Australia's community broadcasting sector. As well as tracing the intellectual path of community media studies, it sets out to locate community broadcasting within broader intellectual debates around notions of community, governance and the media. These are brought back to the "on-the-ground" reality throughout the thesis by means of policy analysis, interviews and anecdotal evidence. Chapters Three to Five map out the themes of access, the public interest and development by reference to community broadcasting in different regions. In North America I explore notions of free speech and first-come-first served models of access. In Europe, notions of "quality", public service broadcasting and the difficult relationship that community broadcasting has with public interest values. Through the Third World and the Third Way I examine how community broadcasting is implicated within development discourse and ideas of social change. The final chapter of the thesis moves into the virtual region of the Internet, looking at changing notions of access and the relevance of new communications rationales to the community broadcasting project. At the intersection of the various themes and models discussed throughout the thesis exists a strong rationale for the future of community broadcasting. Although new technologies may be interpreted as the beginning of the end of community broadcasting, I have argued that in fact it is an idea whose time has come. (Elinor Rennie, 03 Dec 2008 03:50)

CHAPTER 2

National Cable and Telecom Association (NCTA)

The National Cable and Telecom Association (NCTA) represents innovators and creators – an industry building the world's most powerful technology platform and creating exciting content and services that entertain, inform, and inspire consumers every day. Just as technology is transforming media and connectivity is unleashing entertainment, NCTA must adapt to reflect the vibrancy, diversity, and spirit of our members. To bring together diverse perspectives to forge and promote consensus so all our members can continue to drive the industry forward: from policy, to content creation, to delivering compelling consumer experiences. Should we really give back those facilities and anywhere from 1-9 channels in over 1,000 communities across the United States? In addition, there are dozens of institutional networks already operating, many interconnected, many with dark fiber we could harness as bandwidth. You are suggesting giving back the one of the largest public interest networks in the world, built on the ideals of free speech and civic participation.

North American Broadcasters Association (NABA)

The North American Broadcasters Association (NABA) is a non-profit group of broadcasting organizations in the United States, Canada, and Mexico. It is "committed to advancing the interests of broadcasters at home and internationally." As a member of the World Broadcasting

Unions, NABA "creates the opportunity for North American broadcasters to share information, identify common interests and reach consensus on international issues." NABA also provides representation for North American broadcasters in global forums on topics including protection of content, spectrum related concerns, the territorial integrity of broadcasters' signals and digital transition issues. NABA's full members, who represent network broadcasters both public and private, work together with their colleagues including national broadcasting associations, specialty services, service providers and vendors to provide a common voice for the North American broadcast community.

Later, for the community television broadcasters there was the Association for Public, Education & Government Television Stations (APTS) was established in 1979, promoting the legislative and regulatory interests of noncommercial television stations at the national level through direct advocacy and through grass tops and grassroots campaigns designed to garner bipartisan political support. The public television system is comprised of 170 licensees operating more than 350 public television stations across America and serving more than 98 percent of the American people.

The Association for Public, Education & Government Television Stations (APTS)

America's Public Television Stations (APTS) is a nonprofit membership organization ensuring a strong and financially sound public television system and helping member stations provide essential public services in education, public safety, and civic leadership to the American people. Its affiliate APTS Action, Inc. promotes the legislative and regulatory interests of noncommercial television stations at the national level through direct advocacy and through grass tops and grassroots campaigns designed to garner bipartisan political support. The public television system is comprised of 170 licensees operating more than 350 public television stations across America and serving more than 98 percent of the American people. About half of these licensees are nonprofit community foundations. The rest are State, university and local school district licensees. All are locally owned, locally operated and locally oriented in their programming and community services, and all share a mission of serving everyone, everywhere, every day for free – including in places where no model for commercial success exists.

Established in 1979, APTS has been representing Community/ Public television stations nationwide and have been serving America's community or public television its conception in early 1950s, when the Federal Communications Commission reserved a portion of the broadcast spectrum for noncommercial educational purposes. KUHT-TV in Houston was the first public television station to go on the air, in 1952, and Alabama Public Television launched the first statewide public broadcasting network in 1955. President Eisenhower proposed the first federal support for public television in the National Defense Education Act of 1958, to explore the power of television in improving instruction and student outcomes in elementary and secondary schools, and the Public Television Finance Act of 1962 provided federal funds to dramatically expand the number of public television stations in the United States. In 1967, Congress passed the Public Broadcasting Act, establishing the Corporation for Public Broadcasting and creating the modern public broadcasting system.

Public Broadcasting Service (PBS) - UNITED STATES

In 1968 the Dale City, Virginia Jaycees' Junior Chamber of Commerce operated the first community-operated closed-circuit television channel in the United States, when Cable TV Incorporated gave a channel to the public access center, Dale City Television (DCTV), but the center failed two years later. [Today, there are almost 400 public access channels in the United States.] In 1972, the FCC required all cable systems in the top 100 U.S. television markets to provide three access channels, one each for public, educational, and local government use. [Together, these three channels are referred to as PEG access channels.]

The rule was amended in 1976 to include cable systems in communities with 3,500 or more subscribers. But, in 1979 the US Supreme Court, in FCC v. Midwest Video Corp., set aside the FCC's rules as beyond the agency's jurisdiction. The 1984 Cable Franchise Policy and

Communications Act written by Senator Barry Goldwater allowed local governments to require PEG channels, barred cable operators from exercising editorial control over the content of programs carried on PEG channels and absolved them from liability for that content.

Congress passed the Cable Television Consumer Protection and Competition Act of 1992, which gave the FCC authority to create rules requiring cable operators to prohibit certain shows. The Alliance for Community, an advocacy and lobbying organization that supports public access television – and in which Speak Up maintains membership –, and others brought suit, and in 1996 the U.S. Supreme Court held the law unconstitutional, in part because it required cable operators to act on behalf of the federal government to control expression based on content.

Currently, the Alliance for Community Media and others are focusing on operational challenges after new deregulation rules in various states – including Florida – took away local government controls and began directly threatening PEG access in those states. TBCN is now the only public access station left standing in the State of Florida. It is trying to get the Consumer Protection Act of 2007 amended to better protect the PEG channels.

Today, the public television system is comprised of 170 licensees operating more than 350 public television stations across America and serving more than 98 percent of the American people. About half of these licensees are nonprofit community foundations. The rest are State, university and local school district licensees. All are locally owned, locally operated and locally oriented in their programming and community services, and all share a mission of serving everyone, everywhere, every day for free – including in places where no model for commercial success exists. In addition to broadcasting high-quality PBS programming in every American community, America's public television stations are committed to three essential public service missions: education, public safety, and civic leadership.

Public television stations are educational institutions committed to lifelong learning for the American people. This work goes beyond the television, tablet or phone screen and begins with the most successful early childhood education ever devised and continues with unique classroom services and teacher professional development resources, high school equivalency preparation, workforce training and adult enrichment. Public broadcasters have embraced their public safety mission and are focused on maximizing their broadcast spectrum to help keep the public safe in times of emergencies. Public television stations partner with federal, State and local public safety, law enforcement and first responder organizations — connecting these agencies with one another, with the public and with life-saving datacasting services.

Public television regards its viewers as citizens rather than consumers. Public television stations are committed to thorough and thoughtful historical and public affairs programming that provides all Americans with a better understanding of their communities, our country and America's place in the world. Public television stations help citizens and communities understand the issues they face locally and regionally — enabling them to develop solutions based on facts and civil discourse and rooted in community partnerships.

Public broadcasting is an effective public-private partnership. The federal investment in public broadcasting amounts to an annual cost of about $1.35 for each American. This investment compares with $63 per citizen in Japan, $84 in Great Britain. For the 14th consecutive year, the American people have rated public broadcasting as the nation's most trusted institution among nationally known organizations and one of the best values for tax dollars, second only to military defense. This trust extends across the political spectrum: majorities of Democrats, independents and Republicans alike have positive opinions of public broadcasting and support federal funding for it in overwhelming numbers.

This federal funding is the lifeblood of public broadcasting, providing critical seed money to local stations which leverage each $1 of the federal investment to raise over $6 in non-federal financial resources, resulting in a phenomenally successful public-private partnership. President Reagan praised documentary filmmaker Ken Burns for creating such a funding partnership for his landmark public television series The Civil War, and for his commitment to preserving the national memory.

This successful public broadcasting public-private partnership directly supports nearly 20,000 jobs, and almost all of them are in local public television and radio stations in hundreds of communities across America. Public television educates people of all ages, saves American lives, and empowers America's citizens.

However, since the commercial and public television broadcaster's sector's had their advocacy groups, it was in 1976 when the Alliance for Community Media was established to represent public, educational and government access cable TV organizations and community media centers throughout the United States.

Mass media have never guaranteed access by the common man. Throughout history, each new medium seemed to tip the balance of equal expression further in favor of the wealthy elite. Literacy gave the written word to those who could afford an education. Newspapers, magazines, radio, and television have had exclusive ownership, and paid advertising as a means of personal expression has been hindered by high rates. Even the notion of publicly owned airwaves has never guaranteed people automatic access to them. The common man's traditional forum has often been a soapbox in the town-square - a strong voice on a busy street corner.

Today, the corner teeming with pedestrians is dying, replaced by shopping malls whose corporate owners prohibit protesters and orators. But in many communities with cable television, the common man has a new soapbox - one from which his voice can potentially reach thousands of cable subscribers. Public access TV, also called cable access, community access, community television, and PEG (Public, Education and Government), is a system that provides television production equipment, training and airtime on a local cable channel, so members of the public can produce their own shows and televise them to a mass audience. In the United States, public access depends on the cable medium. Community Antenna Television began in Astoria, Oregon, when L. E. Parsons erected an antenna atop the hotel in which he lived to receive the broadcasts of KRSC-TV in Seattle, Washington. He later extended service to the hotel lobby, then to a nearby music store, and later to residences (Gillespie, 20).

The Television Broadcasters Associations (CBA)

In the beginning of establishing local community television broadcast stations in different cities in the United States. It had a national association that lobbied to the United States federal government. It was called The Community Broadcast Association (CBA). The CBA was a trade organization representing low power broadcasting interests, including Low Power TV (LPTV) and Class A television stations, in the United States of America. Class A stations are denoted by the broadcast callsign suffix "CA" (analog) or "CD" (digital), although very many analog - CA stations have a digital companion channel that was assigned the LD suffix used by regular (non-class-A) digital LPTV stations. It ceased operations in 2009. Key issues addressed by the CBA included the provision of interference protection for small broadcasters (for which it successfully petitioned the FCC for creation of the "Class A" designation in 1998) and the need for analog passthrough in coupon-eligible converter boxes (it had unsuccessfully pursued legal action claiming that the absence of this feature, needed to avoid blocking signals from low-power and foreign stations not converting to digital in 2009, violates the All-Channel Receiver Act of 1961).

CBA's lawsuit seeking an injunction to halt the sale and distribution of DTV converter boxes lacking analog tuners and analog pass-through was filed in March 2008, but denied without comment in the U.S. Court of Appeals for the District of Columbia in May 2008. The FCC and NTIA urged manufacturers to include analogue pass-through voluntarily in all converter boxes, and some of the newest generation of models now offer the feature. Due to the large number of public service announcements on full-service stations, which often confusingly claimed that *"all TV is going digital"* on February 17, 2009, the CBA established websites such as KeepUsOn.com to notify consumers of the continued post-transition operation of analogue LPTV, with information on how to find and install converters which offered analogue pass-through capability. The CBA also advocated that existing Class A stations be permitted to upgrade to full service status, obtaining the same must-carry access to cable television that was available to full-power broadcasters, and (like full-power broadcasters opposed expansion of the FM radio band into the frequency range currently occupied by TV channels 5 and 6. Amy Brown was the executive director of the Community Broadcasters Association when it closed. The corresponding advocacy role for US full-service television stations is filled by the National Association of Broadcasters.

The North American Broadcasters Association (NABA) was established to advancing the interests of broadcasters at home and internationally. Mainly for the United States, Canada, and Mexico. Each year, the NABA holds a Conference & Annual General Meeting (AGM). This event provides members with the opportunity to gather in one place to discuss important issues in official meetings and through conference panels. NABA members host each event at their facilities, with the most recent AGMs taking place at CNN (Atlanta), Fox (Los Angeles), CBC/Radio-Canada (Toronto), NBC-Universal (New York), Televisa/TV Azteca (Mexico City) and NPR (Washington, DC).

The Alliance for Community Media

The Alliance for Community Media is an educational, advocacy and lobbying organization in the United States which represents public, educational, and government access cable TV organizations and community media centers throughout the country. Founded in 1976, the Alliance represents over 3,000 public, educational, and governmental (PEG) access organizations and community media center throughout the country. The ACM works to protect the interests of these access centers and those who use PEG facilities and equipment to advance their causes through cable television and the Internet. We also represent:

o   Local community groups
o   Public schools
o   Religious institutions
o   Colleges and universities
o   Government officials
o   Second language communities
o   National institutions such as NASA, the US Department of Education, and the US Army

ACM Mission

The Alliance for Community Media is a national membership organization that advocates, promotes and preserves the right to media training, production, distribution, civic engagement and education in support of diverse community voices, through Public, Educational and Government Access channels and other forms of media.

ACM's Vision

All communities have the resources, ability and right to express themselves, create community dialogue and engage in civic life through local media.

Guiding Principles

Promote free speech, expand civic engagement through local media, collaborate with others, and act with one voice.

The Canadians

Public access began long before television, when Canadian filmmaker Robert Flaherty allowed an Inuit hunter to participate in the production decisions of what became the first documentary (ibid, 27). "Nanook of the North" was released in 1922, but it would be an inspiration to a group of Canadian filmmakers in the 1960s. The National Film Board of Canada (NFB) experimented with a project called Challenge for Change, a documentary film series that was part of Canada's "War on Poverty." people According to David Gee, Secretary of the Interdepartmental Committee of the Challenge for Change program, its purpose was "to create in Canadians an awareness of the need for change in order that [people] may achieve a better quality of life. The film medium permits not only to become aware of problems facing them in their society, but of government programs that can offer real solutions to these problems" (ibid, 23).

The first Challenge for Change documentary, "September 5 at Saint-Henri," went into distribution amidst "extremely negative" reactions on the part of its subjects, who suffered ridicule from their neighbors. One family was so affected that they considered pulling their children from the local school (ibid, 21). When the NFB assigned filmmaker Fernand Dansereau to a similar project in December 1966, he permitted each of the documentary's subjects (excluding politicians) to view the uncompleted film during production and editing and to censor objectionable material. He had not planned this process from by "accident" (ibid, 22).

In 1967, the Challenge for Change crew went to Newfoundland's Fogo Island. The the start, but said it happened decline of the fishing industry had forced 60% of the 5,000 inhabitants into poverty. They lived in ten isolated, mutually antagonistic settlements. The film crew had intended to promote social change by producing documentaries focused on specific issues (Gillespie, 24-25, Engelman, 8-10). They modified the plan because the islanders preferred short films limited to a single interview or event (Engelman, 8). The NFB's web site lists 27 Fogo Island films, ranging in length from less than seven minutes to about 28 minutes. Titles include "Discussion on Welfare," "Joe Kinsella on Education," "The Songs of Chris Cobb" and "William Wells Talks about the Island" (Series List). The inhabitants helped select the film topics. These films had a direct impact on the Fogo Island community. For example, the people had failed to convince the provincial government to create a cooperative fish-processing plant until cabinet ministers saw the films (Engelman, 8-10).

When Sony introduced the video Porta-Pak in 1968, filmmakers Bonny Klein and Dorothy Hénaut convinced Challenge for Change to use it for community projects similar to Fogo Island. (ibid, 11-12) The NFB was at first reluctant. The new half-inch video system had its drawbacks: It could not at that time be transferred to two-inch video, it was not compatible with the 16 millimeter projectors that were standard in schools, and its low resolution confined it to a small screen. But its advantages of portability, low cost, and "simplicity of operation" opened the filmmaking process to non-filmmakers (ibid, 12). In 1968, Hénaut and Klein went to a Montreal Slum where they trained members of the St. Jacques Citizens' Committee in video production. The committee members interviewed poor people and presented their tapes at public meetings. From 1969 to 1970, Challenge for Change co-sponsored a video project with the University of Calgary's School of Social Welfare.

In Alberta's Rosedale village, which "lacked local government, water, sewers, and gas," members of the Rosedale Citizens' Action Committee were trained "to tape interviews with residents about local problems." More than half the Rosedale residents viewed the interviews at a community center, after which they formed committees to address specific problems. This led to local efforts and negotiations with business and government resulting in a new factory "and the installation of gas and water lines" (ibid, 13).

Hénaut and Klein had expressed hopes in 1968 that community-produced video could be merged with cable TV. In 1970, Challenge for Change supplied video equipment and training to Town Talk, a civic organization in Thunder Bay, Ontario. Town Talk also obtained four hours a week on the local cable system for community programming and began cablecasting on November 9. A lack of support and charges that radicals controlled the project doomed it to failure (Engelman, 15; Gillespie, 33-34). But Hénaut said, "the lessons learned . . . are important guides for future development in the theory and practice of citizen access to media" (Gillespie, 34). Other public access experiments soon followed. In the Lake St. John area of Quebec, "the school system assumed considerable responsibility" for community television, in which ten percent of the population became involved. Eventually, on July 16, 1971, the Canadian Radio and Television Commission required cable companies to provide public access channels (Engelman, 16).

The North Americans

The Dale City (Virginia) Junior Chamber of Commerce operated what a Rand report said, "appears to be the first community-operated closed-circuit television channel in the United States." In 1968, Cable TV, Incorporated, provided a channel for the public access center (Gillespie, 35-36), but poor financing, low-quality equipment and lack of a permanent studio contributed to the center's failure two years later (ibid, 36, 59).

GUERRILLA TELEVISION

In the 1960s and 1970s, counter-culture video collectives with names like Videofreeks, Video Free America and Global Village worked to extend the role of the underground press to new communication technologies. Michael Shamberg, Paul Ryan and other video enthusiasts co-founded a video collective called Raindance Corporation (Engelman, 24). Paul Ryan had been a student and research assistant of Marshall McLuhan (ibid, 25), who believed modern technology, such as television, was creating a global village and challenging cultural values (Playboy). Ryan coined the term "cybernetic guerrilla warfare" to describe how the counter-culture movement of the late 1960s and early 1970s should use communication technology to get its message to the public (Engelman, 26). Despite an anti-technology bias in the counter-culture movement, people like Ryan and former Time-Life correspondent Michael Shamberg believed new technology held hope for social change (ibid, 26). According to Shamberg, "cybernetic guerrilla warfare" meant "restructuring communications channels, not capturing existing ones" (ibid, 28).

But Shamberg preferred the term "Guerrilla Television" (the title of his 1971 book), because despite its strategies and tactics similar to warfare, guerrilla television is non-violent (Shamberg II, p. 8). He also saw Guerrilla Television as a means to break through the barriers imposed by broadcast television, which he called "beast television" (Shamberg I, p. 32). Shamberg provided the example of NBC commentator Sander Vanocur broadcasting from a platform above a crowd of demonstrators in Washington, D.C. contrasted with a Raindance video shot within the crowed, allowing people to "speak for themselves." "Guerrilla Television is grassroots television," he wrote. "It works with people, not from up above them" (Shamberg II, p. 8). He urged combining the video Porta-Pak and cable TV to permit ordinary people to communicate a diversity of opinions to their communities (Engelman, 26-27). Shamberg wrote, "The inherent potential of information technology can restore democracy in America if people will become skilled with information tools" (ibid, 28).

NEW YORK

According to Engelman, public access in New York was conceived in 1968 by Fred Friendly, a television advisor to the Ford Foundation and chairman of Mayor John Lindsay's Advisory Task Force on CATV and Telecommunications. He wrote a report recommending that cable companies set aside two channels the public could lease for a minor fee (ibid, 32).

Controversy peaked on July 23, 1970, just prior to the signing of a cable television franchise agreement, when actor Ossie Davis and Cliff Frazer, director of a community film workshop, criticized the agreement for not providing "sufficient participation by minorities." Others opposed the fee requirements, which were eventually dropped (ibid, 32-33).

Two cable companies signed the franchise agreement with the New York City government in July 1970 to supply cable service to Manhattan (Gillespie, 36; Engelman, 32). The agreement required that Sterling Information Services and the Teleprompter Corporation make four channels available for lease - two by the city government and two by the public. Public access programming began a year later in July 1971, with a potential audience of 80,000 - the number of cable subscribers in Manhattan (Engelman, 33). Eventually, the two public access channels were cablecasting about 200 hours of programming each week (ibid, 34).

In 1971 was also the year WGBH foundation in Boston began a nightly half-hour show called "Catch 44," on which they allowed any local group "to air its views free-of-charge." WGBH also encouraged participants to experiment with half-inch video equipment to produce segments for the show (ibid, 3-4).

Back in Manhattan, once the access channels were operational, programming was needed. Theadora Sklover established Open Channel to produce programs and to promote access use by others in the community. The Markle Foundation and the Stern Fund awarded grants to Open Channel to provide production facilities and to hire personnel who would help groups produce shows.

Sklover had previously lobbied the New York State Legislature to pass a bill that would create public access. "At the time she established Open Channel," she wrote that if public access "fails, if these channels are not used, or if they carry programming that no one cares about..., or if they are utilized for the entertainment of the esoteric few, then we probably will have provided the necessary fuel for those who are fighting against the opening of this medium." Once she began facing the reality of promoting access channel use, Sklover said, "our biggest problem lies in informing the public that they can go on television.... People are used to thinking of TV as something someone else does, not as something they do." (ibid, 33).

Sklover identified constituencies, organized local cable committees and trained citizens to use video equipment. She brought in over 200 professional TV and film producers, directors, writers, camera operators, audio specialists, and lighting technicians to volunteer their expertise for public access programming. Open Channel arranged air-time for groups "ranging from the Boy Scouts to black militants, from the Museum of Modern Art to church choirs." In 1972, Sklover articulated the free speech mission of community television: "We're not here to editorialize or make decisions about what people can say over the air" (Newsweek, Engelman, 34).

Open Channel was one of five groups that facilitated public access productions (Engelman, 34). The others were John Reilley's Global Village, which became a leading supplier of documentaries; Raindance Corporation; People's Video Theater, which "captured untraditional forms of reportage and agitprop on videotape;" and the Alternative Media Center, which received $10,000 in equipment from Sterling Information Services for access producers (Engelman, 34; Gillespie, 37).

George Stoney, an American who had been "guest executive producer of Challenge for Change from 1968 to 1970," co-founded the Alternative Media Center (AMC) at New York University in 1971 with Red Burns, a Canadian filmmaker trained at the NFB. The purpose of AMC was to ensure "that new communication technologies serve the public interest" (Engelman, 18). George Stoney's experience at Challenge for Change may have been instrumental in AMC's use of video to resolve citizens' conflicts with local authorities. AMC's documentary of a neighborhood's need for a street light, for example, bears a resemblance to the Fogo Island fish-processing plant campaign mentioned earlier (ibid, 9-10; 34).

Many consider Stoney, who is today the Paulette Goddard Professor in Film at New York University (New York University), the "father of public access television in the United States" (Engelman, 19). AMC was not only instrumental in production, but also in policymaking. AMC founded the National Federation of Local Cable Programmers, which remains an important public access advocacy organization; it's "interns helped establish access centers throughout the nation;" and Stoney and Red Burns worked with FCC commissioner Nicholas Johnson to create the FCC cable access requirements in 1972 (ibid, 19).

REGULATION AND FRANCHISING

Advocates for public access TV won a victory in 1972 when the FCC issued its Third Report and Order, which required all cable systems in the top 100 U.S. television markets to provide three access channels, one each for educational, local government and public use. If there was insufficient demand for three in a market, the cable companies could offer fewer channels, but at least one. Any group or individual wishing to use the channels was guaranteed at least five minutes free. The cable companies were also required to provide the facilities and equipment with which people could produce shows (Gillespie, 91; Hollowell vol. 3, p.103; FCC...).

In 1976 the rule was amended to include cable systems in communities with 3500 or more subscribers. The cable companies had no discretion. Midwest Video Corporation then sued the FCC on the grounds that it had overstepped its authority in requiring the access channels. The Supreme Court, in 1979, ruled in favor of Midwest (FCC...). This was a blow to supporters of community television, since the wording of many cable franchise agreements had relied on the FCC's order to create access channels in their communities (Hollowell vol.2, p. 107).

By the time of the ruling, however, some local governments had written franchise agreements requiring cable companies to provide an access channel irrespective of FCC rules. Baldwin defines a franchise as a contract between the city and a cable company that defines the conditions under which cable service will be provided to the community (Balwin, 204).

Hollowell describes examples of franchise agreements negotiated between 1978 and 1980 in New York State. In 1979, White Plains, a town of only 20,000 people at the time, required the local cable franchise to provide four access channels. In Rochester, the franchisee agreed to provide $100,000 for access production equipment and up to $83,100 a year for staff for five years. In Syracuse, the franchise required an access center and a three-person staff (Hollowell, Vol. 2, pp. 110-111).

In Eau Claire, Wisconsin, an advisory committee recommended to the city council, in September 1977, that a public access center be established as part of the new cable TV franchise agreement. The access center budget was proposed to the city council in October and $10,000 was approved for 1978. Meanwhile, Wisconsin CATV secured an agreement from the L. E. Phillips Memorial Public Library to provide studio space in its basement. Wisconsin CATV purchased and installed production equipment for access use. In January 1978, the Public Access Board convened for the first time, and in March the new Eau Claire Public Access Center began producing local shows ranging "from City Council meetings to individual poetry programs" (PACT).

While the Supreme Court's 1979 Midwest Video decision discouraged community TV supporters, the 1984 Cable Franchise Policy and Communications Act restored much of what had been lost. Senator Barry Goldwater wrote the act, which allowed local governments to require "public, educational or government" (PEG) channels (Sec. 611 - Baldwin, 384-385). It also barred cable operators from exercising editorial control over content of programs carried on PEG channels and absolved them from liability for that content (Sec. 638, 639 - Baldwin, 407, 180; Roberts), which addressed the free speech mission of an institution often shrouded in controversy.

A year earlier, the Public Access Center (PAC) in Eau Claire, Wisconsin, was criticized for televising a tape produced by a man convicted of murdering a city police officer. Christian Bangert produced his tape while free on bail, claiming the local media's version of events would prevent him from getting a fair trial. On October 6, 1982, Bangert had been arguing with his girlfriend when Officer Robert Bolton responded to the domestic abuse call. In a struggle with Bangert, Bolton was fatally shot.

Bangert pleaded no-contest and the video was shown in court at his sentencing hearing and several times on PAC's cable channel. Eau Claire Police Chief James McFarlane considered the airing of the show an insult and said it "was in poor taste." Robert Shaw, a member of the City Council (which had contributed $40,000 to PAC), said that while the City Council should not decide what programs air on PAC, the facility's executive director should (Lautenshlager, 1A, 2A).

Around the country, explicit sex and promotion of Nazi groups have also appeared on PEG channels. To protect children from indecent programming, Congress passed the Cable Television Consumer Protection and Competition Act of 1992. This law gave the FCC authority to create rules requiring cable operators to prohibit certain shows. When the FCC drew up such rules, the Alliance for Community Media and others sued (Roberts).

In 1996, the U.S. Supreme Court held the law unconstitutional, in part because it required cable operators to act on behalf of the federal government to control expression based on content. According to Justices Kennedy and Ginsburg, "Where the government thus excludes speech from a public forum on the basis of its content, the Constitution requires that the regulation be given the most exacting scrutiny" (Denver Area...).

Public access television is not at all restricted to the United States and Canada. Today, it can be found in such places as the United Kingdom, New Zealand, Denmark, Fiji, South Africa, Austria, etc. (Global Village CAT). In Germany, Kanal Dortmund began operating in June 1985 (Small History). In Brazil, Law 8.977 of June 1, 1995, "requires cable operators to make available" six channels free "for public use, to ensure the exercise of free speech" (História; Legislação).

Through history, the common man has struggled for equal expression in the face of greater advantage flowing to the wealthy elite. This trend has left the common man with no forum but a soapbox on a dying street corner. Today, political will and new technologies, like portable video and cable television, have combined to give the common man a new soapbox - one which, despite attempts to control it, is spreading round the world.

-- Eau Claire, Wisconsin, April 3 to May 12, 2000

CHAPTER 3

What does the Future look like for Community Television Broadcaster's?

With the Association for Public, Education & Government Television Stations (APTS) was established to function as the advocates for the United States local government, education and community television industry, where community television broadcaster fall under the third tier of the television broadcasters. It is not known that all the local community television broadcast stations are membership based on the national CTV advocate association. APTS also offer grants:

Linda K Fuller, in her book *Community Television in the United States*, describes community television in terms of its history, its technical characteristics, and its legal, economic, political, and social concerns, highlighting the work of more than 150 related organizations and local television efforts from 100 cities and towns. Linda K. Fuller, in her book, analyzes how competing exigencies and emerging communication technologies might threaten access in the future. Students, scholars, and professionals in television, communications, and public policy will find this reference a definitive one.

With the introduction of the Internet, smart TV's tablets, streaming boxes and devices, and cell phones there have only a few local community television broadcasters' who have access, capability or means to broadcast over these new systems. However, there are a few with larger groups can use these additional media systems necessary to reach not only their local audience but international. Even with its national representative the America's Public Television Stations (APTS). Can the APTS maintain the feasibility of local community television broadcaster's placement in the three-tier television broadcast industry.

The Future of Local Public Access Television Stations

In this era of global and social media, you can get a taste of what is going on in every corner of the world. However, some of the best happenings are right in your own backyard, local government, local sports and school activities and everyday interesting people and events in your city. Coverage of all this activity keeps people informed and entertained where they live. Public access television has historically been a viable way to provide communities with non-mainstream programming. To support local programming The Cable Communications Act of 1984 was created, giving a local town or city government, the authority to require a cable operator to provide television channels that are designated for Public, Educational and Government use, called "PEG" for short. The number of designated stations, their funding and who will run them is listed in a 10-15-year franchise agreement, between the cable provider and the locale that is usually negotiated through a series of public meetings. Also, a franchise fee, which by law can be no greater than 5 percent of the television portion of your monthly cable bill, provides the funding for PEG channels.

Beginning in the 1980s, cable providers usually built, equipped, and managed the studio while training residents on how to utilize equipment and produce their own shows. In general, residents did not have much input into the day-to-day operation of PEG stations and in the New England states, a couple of mergers and buyouts negatively impacted local PEG stations. In the mid-2000s, many of the 10-15-year franchise agreements were coming up for renewal. At the time, Comcast made it clear that it wanted to put the day –to-day operation of PEG channels and local access studios into the hands of the local community. As part of the renewal contract, the PEGs were required to establish the station as a non-profit organization to operate. The franchise fee that Comcast collected would then be sent directly to the cities for the support of the PEG non-profit.

By being an independent non-profit, PEGS now operated with a board of directors and the flexibility to quickly make decisions regarding viewership and membership, without the longer processes in dealing with the local, states or federal government. A prime example of a successful public access television station is San Francisco's KQED (PBS station), which was overseen by the government but transitioned into non-profit leadership. A weekly formula of covering an event one week and airing it the next week is what many PEGs follow when videotaping on-location local youth sports, concerts, and other community events. Locals seeing locals on television usually piques the interest of even more aspiring producers. Oakland has two educational channels KDOL TV and a government channel KTOP but No community access channel.

According to Bishop, J.E. Watkins, Founder/CEO of OWH Studios, (Overcomers with Hope Studios), a local 501c3 television production studio that trains at risk youth, young adults and veterans in Television/Broadcast Digital Arts Media, Oakland is missing a huge opportunity that is not being utilized. *"Funding is earmarked for PEG stations,"* said Watkins. *"Why doesn't Oakland have a public access channel?"* Watkins also says there is an annual budget in the City of Oakland that is not used each year for a public access television station. Watkins states he has been asking the question of the City of Oakland and council members for several years now as he has built a first-class state of the art broadcast ready studio in West Oakland in the historic Marcus Garvey Building. "With donated state of the art 2K and 4K equipment, students are trained on the latest technology available to create broadcast quality programming for air right now at OWH," he said. *"This creates jobs and opportunity for people living right here."* With a robust training program, modern equipment, and a community of dedicated volunteers, Watkins feels OWH is well prepared to fill the public access void in Oakland. With his team of industry professional producers, directors, videographers, and a library of locally produced shows to air, he hopes his dream of expanding opportunity in Oakland's media and exposure to the world can be fulfilled.

Part II of this article will focus on OWH Studios, the lives it has transformed with its training program and the need for a public access channel in Oakland.

Jason Crow Interview with Professor Dan Gillmor

Professor Dan Gillmor being interviewed on an online article on February 21, 2007 by Jason Crow, titled "Beyond Broadcast: Future of Public Access TV" *"I think it's time to phase out public-access TV and replace it with something more attuned to the Internet Age, and I wrote a blog posting to that effect. Jason has his doubts about this, to put it mildly, and has interjected some comments in my posting.* Dan Gillmor is an American technology writer and columnist. He is director of the Knight Center for Digital Media Entrepreneurship at Arizona State University's Walter Cronkite School of Journalism and Mass Communication and a fellow at the Berkman Center for Internet & Society at Harvard University. Gillmor is also the author of a popular weblog covering technology news and the Northern California technology business sector, criticizing rigid enforcement of copyrights, and commenting on politics from a liberal perspective.

DAN GILLMOR: Day and night across America, cable television systems devote one of their channels to programming known as "Public Access" — shows created by people in the communities the cable companies serve. The programs range from interesting and useful to dull and dreadful. That is what you would expect from material created by people who aren't media professionals. (Which is not to say that the pros create only great things themselves, of course.) Good too bad to ugly, public access cable TV has given voice to people who had something to say. Using the cable companies' production facilities and distribution, these folks have been able to make themselves heard by anyone who cared to watch and listen. Public access, by almost any standard, has been a valuable addition to the local media scene. Valuable, but outdated: It is time to phase out public access — but in a way that brings us even better publicly created news and entertainment. The cable companies do not like it. They must spend money to provide it, dollars they're much rather send to their bottom lines and shareholders. It costs bandwidth they would rather use for other programming.

JASON CROW: The telephone companies trying to enter the business like it even less. They have been working in Washington — lobbying for legislation and revised FCC regulations — and in state capitals for permission to abandon many of their public interest obligations.

DAN GILLMOR: When cable systems were essentially the only game in town for video news and entertainment, their desires carried less weight against the public-interest value of public access. But in the age the Internet and more competitive media, the balance has shifted. I am not suggesting that we let the cable companies simply walk away from their community obligations. But there's a fine way to give them relief from the burden of public access while increasing the number of public voices on matters of community interest.

Let us make a deal with them, as follows:

1. In five years, cable systems will be free to abandon public access programming in every way. They will not have to provide production facilities or channels.

JASON CROW: Wow, what you are suggesting is a big giveaway to the cable and telephone companies. Remember, cable companies pay rent for use of public rights of way. At its core, public access TV is a result of a return on the use of public land. According to the National Cable and Telecom Association, cable companies pay $2.8 billion per year in franchise fees – rent for use of public land. These franchises pay the rent for hundreds of public access media center buildings, grant money for equipment, require universal buildout and provide analog channel and digital spectrum allocation.

The National Cable and Telecom Association (NCTA) represents innovators and creators – an industry building the world's most powerful technology platform and creating exciting content and services that entertain, inform, and inspire consumers every day. Just as technology is transforming media and connectivity is unleashing entertainment, NCTA must adapt to reflect the vibrancy, diversity, and spirit of our members. To bring together diverse perspectives to forge and promote consensus so all our members can continue to drive the industry forward: from policy, to content creation, to delivering compelling consumer experiences. Should we really give back those facilities and anywhere from 1-9 channels in over 1,000 communities across the United States? In addition, there are dozens of institutional networks already operating, many interconnected, many with dark fiber we could harness as bandwidth. You are suggesting giving back the one of the largest public interest networks in the world, built on the ideals of free speech and civic participation.

DAN GILLMOR: 2. In the meantime, they will use those production facilities and public-access personnel — who will need some retraining — to help members of the community learn modern media production techniques. Those techniques will focus on a Web model of content, not a broadcast model.

JASON CROW: I propose a *"United Stations"* movement that includes networking all of the stations into one solid network. There are many implications to this:

    a. The largest cable network in the world;
    b. Sharing of resources – curriculum, best practices;
    c. Single marketing entity – dissolve the negative stereotypes;
    d. Share programming (there is tons of good stuff out there).

We need to combine efforts for a net-based, many-to-many media with cable, one-to-many playback– more a Current.tv distribution model, with user submissions, voting, feedback, comments and the best get played on the channels.

DAN GILLMOR: Let us look at the various constituencies of public access and see who gets what under such a deal. Cable companies: Over time, they get out of an obligation they meet grudgingly in most cases. Public access employees: They effectively get a five-year employment guarantee, plus retraining in a field that is in many ways the future of media. The public (the most important constituency): We get a vast array of new programming of all kinds, from a cadre of newly trained citizen media creators. Maybe cable systems will want to put some of it on their channels, or maybe not. But the Web makes it unimportant whether they do or not.

JASON CROW: What about those people who don't have access to broadband?

DAN GILLMOR: Keep in mind that at least some public-access operations are already doing such things. For example, Cambridge (Mass.) Community Television offers a variety of classes with a distinctly Web-ish tint in many cases. Consider the session entitled "ZIP DOCS: 021XX" — the purpose of which is to "map the Cambridge community with video" using such tools as Google. APTS as well as standard video techniques. Cool stuff, and a major part of the future.

JASON CROW: We have offered podcasting and videoblogging classes in the past as well. We suggest our community members tag their content "CCTV Cambridge" in YouTube and Blip for redistribution on our drupal-based web community. I would suggest taking a look at the other progressive institutions around the US. For instance, DeProduction manages Denver Open Media, a public access tv web community that allows user to upload video, rank it, comment on it and get it on the cable channels.

DAN GILLMOR: We need much, much more of this.

Public access television was a good answer for its time. But the era when it was so needed is coming to a close. Let's create a legion of citizen media people who do solid, honorable work for the medium of the future: The Net.

JASON CROW: Let's not abandon 30 years of building infrastructure and creating human connections with municipal leaders. We don't have to reinvent the system, just adapt it to new technologies. There are great citizen journalists on the web like Lisa Williams who benefit from her Selectmen meeting being broadcast on her Government Access channel. She posts excerpts to her placeblog via YouTube. Let's follow this example and work together to create a United Stations movement.

The Future of the Local Community Broadcast TV

Mr. Craig Reed in his online article titled, "Beyond-broadcast strategies key to survival of local public TV stations." February 28, 2017 Henry Ford said, "If I had asked my customers what they wanted, they would have said 'faster horses.'" Just as Ford revolutionized transportation by developing assembly-line manufacturing of automobiles, today's most successful entrepreneurs invented internet-based technologies that disrupted how we do business and communicate. Their innovations require all of us in media to rethink how we connect to audiences and earn revenues.

It is not just us media types who are perplexed. In a recent *Harvard Business Review* article, "Are You Solving the Right Problems?", 85 percent of business executives agreed that their organizations had difficulty discerning what were the crucial problems confronting their companies. In a sense, some businesses are trying to find faster horses when the threat and its solution lies elsewhere. We have been thinking about how disruptions to the media ecosystem affect local public television stations, and solutions that will help them prepare for the next wave of technological upheavals.

New Television/Video Ecosystem

Let us start with the basics in the media ecosystem: 21st-century broadcasting has evolved from a commercial medium introduced in the 1920s. Since modern broadband internet began 25 years ago, waves of technology and entrepreneurial innovation — the success of Amazon, Netflix, Apple TV, and smartphones, to name a few big ones — have disrupted many 20th-century business models. Turner Broadcasting's John Martin introduced a convenient analogy that sums up how the internet changed that TV ecosystem: a three-legged stool.

Before the advent of the internet, the mantra in the media business was "Content is king." During that era huge production costs were barriers for anyone who wanted to produce movies, television series or music albums. And there were unbreachable barriers to content distribution. You needed movie theaters, broadcast stations or record stores to reach audiences. Now, however, the first leg of the stool — content — is much cheaper to produce, and the sheer amount available has exploded. Distribution, the second leg, is easier because consumers can access programs through the internet. "Over-the-top" internet streaming businesses (Apple TV, Roku, Amazon Prime, Netflix) created new markets using these readily accessible avenues of distribution. Even Facebook is streaming live video. These many venues for content distribution have emerged and disrupted the old ecosystem in less than a decade.

Which brings us to the stool's third leg: the consumer's viewing experience. The explosion of content and new channels of distribution has given viewers more choices. Niche cable channels emerged (think BBC America, Cloo, Oxygen) because people were willing to pay handsomely for more choices. HBO demonstrated that people would pay even more money to escape ads. Netflix, Amazon, and Hulu allowed consumers to decide when *they* wanted to watch a program, instead of ceding that decision to a network programmer. The availability of content on-demand became especially important to the consumer experience. It opened the door to new program packages like skinny bundles and even encouraged cord cutting. For public broadcasters, the ability to manage all three legs of the video ecosystem presents new challenges. There's no school for this; we are all learning to cope with these changes in programming, distribution and viewer satisfaction as we go.

Platform Business on the Internet

The viewer experiences provided by linear television programs are vastly different than what consumers have on YouTube and Facebook. Nevertheless, television and these newer media platforms share a key characteristic: All of them subsidize their users. The programming or content that users enjoy is free because someone or something else pays for it. Television broadcasts have always been subsidized by paid advertising. Commercial networks create programs that target and attract audiences and sell airtime — the attention of those audiences — to advertisers. It is a nice two-sided business with a cash side and a user side: Networks and their stations get the cash, and users (viewers) get to watch for free. Public TV's friction is twofold: for viewers, the expectation that broadcast programming is free inhibits their willingness to become customers, or donors; for advertisers, limitations on what they can say inhibits their willingness to purchase underwriting.

But public television stations cannot do business this way because the Public Broadcasting Act prohibits advertising. Federal Communication Commission (FCC) regulations provide some flexibility for advertisers, a.k.a. underwriters, to sponsor broadcasts of noncommercial educational licensees. With a mandate to provide free programming and prohibitions against selling advertising, public television stations had to develop other ways to raise revenue to support their operations. Enter membership and major donor fundraising, foundation and institutional support, and underwriting solicitation. It's a much more complicated model than the simpler model of cash for eyeballs that our commercial cousins enjoy.

21st-Century Business Models

Platform businesses, oversimplified, have three elements: a community or "commons" where producers and consumers meet; a computer infrastructure that manages those interactions in the community; and data that is generated from the various transactions. Uber is a good example of a simple platform business. On one side are customers who need a ride; on the other drivers with cars who are waiting for a fare. Uber owns and runs the internet-based platform that matches riders with drivers. The money side of this platform business is the rider. Uber retains the data and mines it in different ways to extract value and insight from its day-to-day transactions. For many platform businesses, the data they generate are valuable sources of income.

Most people do not think of broadcast stations as internet business platforms. Broadcast stations give away programming but lack the web-powered connectivity, data collection and analysis competency to find and interact with their viewers in the ways that Netflix or Amazon do. In some platform businesses, a singular problem is turning consumers into customers. It's all about getting people who are using their services to spend money. In platform business jargon, "friction" is the term for an impediment that restrains a customer from doing business.

Unpredictable shipping costs create friction for Amazon. Amazon reduced this friction by creating Amazon Prime, a once-a-year fee that guarantees two-day shipping along with some free video and music thrown in. It worked. Right now, Amazon Prime has 63 million subscribers versus Amazon's 19 million non-prime customers. Public TV's friction is twofold: for viewers, the expectation that broadcast programming is free inhibits their willingness to become customers, or donors; for advertisers, limitations on what they can say inhibits their willingness to purchase underwriting. Public broadcasters have developed a platform, albeit a primitive one, that enables them to connect with viewers: the pledge drive. Pledge premiums reduce friction by furnishing a rationalization to support the station through a tangible "gift." But the practice of relying on pledge premiums to earn money has high negative costs (e.g., interrupting the regular schedule for weeks at a time).

Gold in them there Clicks

However, public stations can develop additional and perform using more effective platforms. Using the internet to build platforms that function like YouTube or Facebook, stations can turn metadata about their users into dollars. "Metadata" is another one of those awkward jargon words that can mean a thousand different things depending on who is using it for what purpose. For our purposes, metadata is the "big data" that we collect about our users. Google and Facebook compile data about individual users' search behavior into metadata that they sell to advertisers, who then create ads that follow the users around the internet. Broadcasters have lacked the data-collection and analysis capability to generate useful metadata on viewers/consumers. Podcasters currently have some data about their members — mostly information about contributing patterns — but not in the depth that the internet furnishes. At present, most stations are collecting some data from their websites and social media platforms like Facebook and YouTube. Integration and standardization of that data — in other words, turning it into metadata — is key to the viability of local stations. Knowing more about all of our viewers — not just contributors — will enable us to form deeper relationships with them, better serve their media needs and ultimately request their support in more powerful ways. Fortunately, there are quite several customer-relationship management systems to choose from, and many of them deal with these issues. WGBH has developed a unique iteration, NGO Connect, that adapts the Salesforce software platform for specific problems facing public media stations.

Why Stations need their own Platforms

To keep their licenses, stations must maintain their broadcast services to FCC standards. At the same time stations must adapt to the disruptions created by the internet — those it has already wrought to media consumption and those yet to come. We can see the disruption in audience viewing behavior, which is already changing how stations do business. Viewing of live linear TV is declining. These days the elderly (65+) constitute much of the linear TV audience.

- Most audience shifts appear first in younger generations and then diffuse to older cohorts. Because older people prefer linear and live TV, public television's audience might seem secure, but that view is shortsighted. See how people aged 49 and younger are spending so much less time with traditional TV? That does not bode well for our audience stability in the coming decade or two. Stations need to adapt to competition from internet and OTT providers because broadcast audiences will keep shrinking. The internet will enable more companies to develop more complex programming platform businesses. Stations may have to clone an "internet platform/station" and collect metadata that can eventually be turned into financial support. Long-held assumptions about the loyalty and passion of the public television viewer will require readjusting. The heaviest, almost addicted viewers of CBS, PBS or TBS, for example, are very old and not very donative. The passionate, loyal and committed public TV viewers and members are very light viewers of all television. They are loyal but infrequent viewers of their local PTV stations. Specific program genres are the trigger for their passion and donations, not viewing frequency. (By: Lynn Leahey, December 7, 2017)

Community Access TV Reluctant to Change

Mr. Jay Dedman explained that currently, some community access centers are reluctant to branch into new media out of fear that offering such services might breach their contract with cable companies. Dedman noted that cable providers are reinventing themselves as broadband providers and said that savvy public-access stations needed to renegotiate their contracts to "get a piece of whatever was going over the wires" — to ensure that cable companies wouldn't be able to revoke funding for offering media services beyond TV. Shaw cross has been the forefront of change in public access. He pioneered several innovations to energize viewers about public access, making Denver Open Media channel a leader amongst public-access channels.

"Every show submitted gets posted online," he said. "Viewers are encouraged to vote and comment via the website or using their cell phones. If you visit our site, you'll see that there's a dynamic scroll and if viewers vote or comment, their feedback scrolls across the screen real-time (almost). The most unique thing about our model is that we do not have a scheduling/programming department. The votes and metadata automatically determine the schedule based on a multi-layered algorithm with various rules and parameters. So, it really puts the control in the viewers' hands like never before."

Shaw cross also emphasized the local aspect of public access, where channels are unique to a city. "Commercial media operations cater to national audiences, and it seems to be widely recognized today that there is an underserved need in the public for more local and hyper-local media," he said. "Public-access stations not only provide a community resource designed to address local communications needs, but unlike the YouTubes of the world, provide a physical space where community members can meet, collaborate, and organize."

Public-Access TV Fights for Relevance in the YouTube Age

In an age when it's increasingly easy for amateur filmmakers, citizen journalists, and the general public to distribute videos online, is there any point in having a public-access cable channel? Some argue that public-access television has outlived its usefulness for this reason: Podcasting and online video have effectively eliminated the need to reserve television slots for public comment. In recent years, telecom companies have used this argument with great success to get out of having to contribute public-access funding. Lack of funding and public interest have caused many of these stations around the country to close up shop.

So if public-access dies, should we mourn it? Is there any reason to preserve it when it's so easy to put the same material online? Advocates argue that online media can't entirely take the place of the classic cable-access model, and that TV call-in shows offer a different kind of interactivity that shouldn't go away.

What Is Public-Access TV?

Public-access television came about with the rise of cable television in the late '70s and early '80s. In exchange for the rights to lay cable wires on public land, cable companies were required to donate a portion of their revenue to provide facilities and airtime to allow public comment. (Such agreements are negotiated on a city-by-city basis). The idea was to give voice to ordinary citizens who otherwise wouldn't have access to any media outlets. In 1984, the Cable Franchise Policy and Communications Act prohibited cable operators from exercising any editorial control over public-access channels.

Thus public-access TV mostly became famous for its eccentric personalities and bizarre shows. (A few break-out stars even got their start on public access, like comedian Tom Green and horror hostess Elvira.) But it's also been a venue for serious political and philosophical discussion, a place to find the recorded minutes of your local town hall meeting or school board discussion, as well as a springboard for citizen journalism. In the 1990s, Lisa Hendrick videotaped city council meetings in Marine City, Mich., to expose inappropriate behavior by elected officials. And many public-access stations rebroadcast investigative pieces by Democracy Now, Free Speech TV and Deep Dish TV Network.

Not Everyone Has Computers

At the moment, the most obvious advantage public-access TV has over online video is simple access. It's sometimes easy to forget that not everyone has access to a computer, but the 2008 biennial news consumption survey by the Pew Research Center for the People & the Press found that 46 percent of Americans still get their news and entertainment primarily through television. Tony Shawcross, executive director of Denver Open Media in Denver, and founder of Deproduction, won a grant from the Knight Foundation to create online tools for public-access TV stations (and blogs on Idea Lab about it). Shawcross told me that cable TV still predominates the media landscape. "Cable television viewership is still orders of magnitude higher than online, and the discrepancy is even higher in low-income communities," he said. "Nielsen has a recent report that estimates cable TV viewership at 25-times the prevalence of online media viewership. Low-income communities do not necessarily have cameras, computers and high-speed Internet. Those tools are not ubiquitous, and have low penetration in low-income communities." But this is only a temporary respite for public access. As technology becomes cheaper and more people become plugged in, this gap is slowly but surely narrowing. Even though experts estimate that it could be another 20 years before online video reaches the same audience numbers as cable TV, activists agree that public access will need to find another way to justify its existence.

The Future of the Local Broadcast TV

In an online article, Mr. Jim Long, CEO of Didja, which launched local, live TV streaming service LocalBTV 2 July 2020.

Every day, headlines remind us that the entire television ecosystem is experiencing a massive change. And yet, among the layoffs and mergers, local broadcast television is having a renaissance. By local broadcast, I mean all the channels you can receive in your city by using an antenna, often as many as 60-100 channels. These typically include 8-10 major networks, such as NBC and Univision, and hundreds of independent stations featuring music videos and programming in a myriad of languages, all serving local communities across the country. Antenna-TV uses a wonderful public national asset called the public airwaves, some people think are every bit as precious as our national parks.

So what is changing? Audiences are increasingly demanding more from their viewing experience, from more high-quality content, greater choice, and convenience. And for the first time ever, we have the technology that has the potential to satisfy these demands for years to come. But it has been a long road to get here.

Thirty years ago, the only way to access TV was through antenna-TV, giving us 10 to 15 channels over-the-air for free. We then decided what to watch either by "channel surfing" or using the TV guide magazine we bought at the grocery store. In the 80s and 90s, cablesystems began offering a low-cost way to get better reception of local channels, particularly UHF stations. Soon, new cable-only channels started to appear and households started paying for TV to receive ang a bundle of both cable channels (not available by antenna) and a subset of the antenna TV channels. Cable companies were later joined by satellite and phone companies to offer such cable-bundles, and by 10 or so years ago such a PayTV cable-bundle was used by about 85% of all households with about 10% using antennas.

More recently, the web/internet has become capable of distributing high-quality video, and a third way to watch TV blossomed – streaming-video-on-demand (svod) services like Netflix & Hulu, not to mention new video sources like YouTube and Facebook-Live.

While cable was growing, the country began getting away from visiting local mom-and-pop stores and restaurants to large, national chains. But now the pendulum is swinging back to local services with farm-to-table movements, shop local initiatives, and back to local broadcast TV.

Thanks to cord-cutting and newly formed homes not paying for cable (who never paid cable bundles), cable-bundle homes are now down to about 77% of all homes even with the new cable-bundle services like SlingTV and YouTubeTV, and is projected to drop to 65% or less in homes within the next five years. This means about 40 million homes in the US will be 'cord-free' and will either watch antenna-TV or not receive any live-linear TV at all.

Bet on the former. Antenna sales have been booming the last couple years and Millennials are discovering the simple fun of antenna-TV. So why is this happening?

1. We all love the amazing new programming coming from the broadcast TV networks and the new suppliers like Netflix, Amazon, Hulu.'Binge watching' has become the newest way to watch TV and the country is watching more 'TV programming' than ever before. The availability of SVOD services is one reason for cord-cutting. But while we love binge watching, it is not a casual viewing experience. It has to be planned and often feels like a commitment.

2. Across the nation, communities are looking more and more to local services such as farm-to-table food shopping and local businesses are taking more pride in their local city and local neighborhoods. We now see how local and national complement each other. This is true for TV too. Local broadcast is 'farm-to-table' TV as it not only has national network programming but local news on those network stations and many purely local, independent stations. Stations cater to local bilingual households which like both English and foreign language TV. And antenna-TV often has better picture quality than cable or internet TV.

So what is the result?

1. Millennials and others are discovering the casual fun of channel surfing to discover new programs and be entertained without the commitment of binge watching. How about just a little TV before bed or while in the DMV line.
2. While the web has become a major source for news, more people see that live local news is a critical piece too, especially for timely critical information. Yes, Millennials are realizing this too.
3. TV stations are adding more interesting broadcast TV channels featuring more than just reruns and serving specific audiences with lifestyle content or science fiction and yes, once again, it's Millennials are discovering it all.
4. Businesses are also realizing the public airwaves and broadcast are valuable resources that complement the Internet. It's pretty obvious that if one million households in Chicago are watching the Super Bowl, a broadcast signal is much more efficient and practical than one million separate high bandwidth internet streams. Not long from now, the local broadcast infrastructure will be used to deliver data to devices all over the community (so-called internet of things, IOT), and sending the same data to many phones and laptops at the same time. (see ATSC-3.0)

So broadcast TV and broadcasting is not going away soon, and probably never will. By my estimates, it will likely rise from 10% of households 10 years ago to 25%+ 10 years from now, particularly as it gets modernized via smartphone apps that allow easy access to antenna-TV via smartphones, tablets and laptops. I suppose that is why, even though many smart folks think it is going the way of the "buggy-whip," the value of broadcast stations has not gone down much over the years and is currently getting stronger.

Cable-bundles will still be a big part of TV but as audiences seek greater choice and control over their viewing, they are rediscovering local broadcast and its low-cost, and easy convenience. How fortunate we are to have antenna-TV as a terrific part of our buffet of video programming.

The Cynsiders column is a platform for industry leaders to reach out to colleagues, followers, and the public at large. In their own words and in targeted Q&As, columnists address breaking news, issues of the day, and the larger changes going on in the ever-evolving world of television, video and digital. Cynsiders columns live on Cynopsis' main page and are promoted across all daily newsletters. We welcome readers' comments, queries, and column ideas at Lynn@Cynopsis.com.

Jim Long, *CEO of Didja, which launched local, live TV streaming service Local BTV on 2 July 2020*

Every day, headlines remind us that the entire television ecosystem is experiencing a massive change. And yet, among the layoffs and mergers, local broadcast television is having a renaissance. By local broadcast, I mean all the channels you can receive in your city by using an antenna, often as many as 60-100 channels. These typically include 8-10 major networks, such as NBC and Univision, and hundreds of independent stations featuring music videos and programming in a myriad of languages, all serving local communities across the country. Antenna-TV uses a wonderful public national asset called the public airwaves; some people think are every bit as precious as our national parks.

So, what is changing? Audiences are increasingly demanding more from their viewing experience, from more high-quality content, greater choice, and convenience. And for the first time ever, we have the technology that has the potential to satisfy these demands for years to come. But it has been a long road to get here.

Thirty years ago the only way to access TV was through antenna-TV, giving us 10 to 15 channels over-the-air for free. We then decided what to watch either by "channel surfing" or using the TV guide magazine we bought at the grocery store. In the 80s and 90s, cablesystems began offering a low-cost way to get better reception of local channels, particularly UHF stations. Soon, new cable-only channels started to appear, and households started paying for TV to receive ang a bundle of both cable channels (not available by antenna) and a subset of the antenna TV channels. Cable companies were later joined by satellite and phone companies to offer such cable-bundles, and by 10 or so years ago such a PayTV cable-bundle was used by about 85% of all households with about 10% using antennas.

More recently, the web/internet has become capable of distributing high-quality video, and a third way to watch TV blossomed – streaming-video-on-demand (SVPD) services like Netflix & Hulu, not to mention new video sources like YouTube and Facebook-Live. While cable was growing, the country began getting away from visiting local mom-and-pop stores and restaurants to large, national chains. But now the pendulum is swinging back to local services with farm-to-table movements, shop local initiatives, and back to local broadcast TV.

Thanks to cord-cutting and newly formed homes not paying for cable (who never paid cable bundles), cable-bundle homes are now down to about 77% of all homes even with the new cable-bundle services like SlingTV and YouTubeTV, and is projected to drop to 65% or less in homes within the next five years. This means about 40 million homes in the US will be 'cord-free' and will either watch antenna-TV or not receive any live-linear TV at all. Bet on the former. Antenna sales have been booming the last couple years and Millennials are discovering the simple fun of antenna-TV. So why is this happening?

1. We all love the amazing new programming coming from the broadcast TV networks and the new suppliers like Netflix, Amazon, Hulu.'Binge watching' has become the newest way to watch TV and the country is watching more 'TV programming' than ever before. The availability of SVOD services is one reason for cord cutting. But while we love binge watching, it is not a casual viewing experience. It must be planned and often feels like a commitment.

2. Across the nation, communities are looking more and more to local services such as farm-to-table food shopping and local businesses are taking more pride in their local city and local neighborhoods. We now see how local and national complement each other. This is true for TV too. Local broadcast is 'farm-to-table' TV as it not only has national network programming but local news on those network stations and many purely

local, independent stations. Stations cater to local bilingual households which like both English and foreign language TV. And antenna-TV often has better picture quality than cable or internet TV.

So, what is the result?

1. Millennials and others are discovering the casual fun of channel surfing to discover new programs and be entertained without the commitment of binge watching. How about just a little TV before bed or while in the DMV line.
2. While the web has become a major source for news, more people see that live local news is a critical piece too, especially for timely critical information. Yes, Millennials are realizing this too.
3. TV stations are adding more interesting broadcast TV channels featuring more than just reruns and serving specific audiences with lifestyle content or science fiction and yes, once again, it's Millennials are discovering it all.
4. Businesses are also realizing the public airwaves and broadcast are valuable resources that complement the Internet. It's pretty obvious that if one million households in Chicago are watching the Super Bowl, a broadcast signal is much more efficient and practical than one million separate high bandwidth internet streams. Not long from now, the local broadcast infrastructure will be used to deliver data to devices all over the community (so-called internet of things, IOT), and sending the same data to many phones and laptops at the same time. (see ATSC-3.0)

So broadcast TV and broadcasting is not going away soon, and probably never will. By my estimates, it will likely rise from 10% of households 10 years ago to 25%+ 10 years from now, particularly as it gets modernized via smartphone apps that allow easy access to antenna-TV via smartphones, tablets and laptops. I suppose that is why, even though many smart folks think it is going the way of the "buggy-whip," the value of broadcast stations has not gone down much over the years and is currently getting stronger.

Cable-bundles will still be a big part of TV but as audiences seek greater choice and control over their viewing, they are rediscovering local broadcast and its low-cost, and easy convenience. How fortunate we are to have antenna-TV as a terrific part of our buffet of video programming.

The Cynsiders column is a platform for industry leaders to reach out to colleagues, followers, and the public at large. In their own words and in targeted Q&As, columnists address breaking news, issues of the day, and the larger changes going on in the ever-evolving world of television, video and digital. Cynsiders columns live on Cynopsis' main page and are promoted across all daily newsletters. We welcome readers' comments, queries, and column ideas at Lynn@Cynopsis.com.

What will public TV look like in 2025?

In 2015, host Lauren-Glenn Davitian, channel 17 public broadcast station in Burlington, Vermont, makes note that in the past there were hundreds of community television broadcaster nationwide. But, these have declined since the introduction of the internet. Also, the cable companies are broadcasted in HD channels which many local public television don't have the capacity to run HD. The cable service providers are not allowing most over the air public broadcast television use of their HD channels, i.e. COMCAST, etc. Also, a lot of cable networks are not putting the public broadcast station's on their channel lineup. Which it makes difficult to any person looking for a public television television show. They are not able to see their local public television TV shows highlighted in mainstream directories.

The fact that Mark Zuckerberg was in his dorm room founding Facebook just 12 years ago should give us pause about predicting too far into the future. Nevertheless, we must try. Here is our best guess of what the ecosystem will look like in eight years. Many stations will have upgraded to ATSC 3.0 (A/300:2017, "ATSC 3.0 System" This Standard describes the ATSC 3.0 digital television system. ATSC 3.0 is a suite of voluntary technical Standards and Recommended Practices that is fundamentally different from predecessor ATSC systems and is therefore largely incompatible with them). The menu-driven viewing paradigm popularized by Netflix and Amazon will have become dominant, and ATSC 3.0 will bring that menu-driven capability to broadcast stations as well as OTT (Over the top (OTT) is a term used to refer to content providers that distribute streaming media as a standalone product directly to viewers over the Internet, bypassing telecommunications, multichannel television, and broadcast television platforms that traditionally act as a controller or distributor of such content.) services. Menu-driven access will be possible for local content as well as national programs. The broadcast schedule will likely still be with us, though, as a clickable viewing option alongside a menu of on-demand programs. Other capabilities of ATSC 3.0 open additional opportunities for public television stations, such as the ability to send related content to "second screens," like smartphones and tablets in the home. Stations will be able to interact with viewers through surveys. With a few tweaks, public television can be well-positioned for this platform world. Children's programming is a crucial necessity for any programming service, and public television has this well in hand. Netflix and other similar services spend significant sums on children's programs. Public television has been in the children's programming business for quite some time and the trust that parents have in our content, proven to be of educational value and free from commercial messages, is a key advantage.

In the internet platform world, it is best to conceive of two programming models for local community broadcast stations. The programming that attracts viewers to a station is common to both. Broadcast schedules will be pretty much like today, a legacy service that some consumers continue to use. However, your platform-based program service will resemble that of Netflix or Amazon. Platform management will be less about "scheduling" and more about warehousing programs, long-tail management and collecting tons of metadata about viewers. Stations will mine that metadata to convert consumers into customers (or viewers into members, for the old-timers) and generate station income. To do this, though, we will need to acquire program rights for a long, long time. The longer we have the rights to keep the content in our warehouse, the better we can mine the metadata to extract value. The local station's future is *beyond broadcasting* programs and into the ether. When broadcasting began as a mass medium, Herbert Hoover was president. The rise of manufacturing and consumerism that produced the Ford Model T and Sears Roebuck has given way to internet-enabled hyper connectivity that fuels Twitter and Amazon.

TRAC (Trac is an enhanced wiki and issue tracking system for software development projects. Trac uses a minimalistic approach to web-based software project management) and Public Media Company have been developing tools and strategies for local stations to use in this ecosystem through TRAC Locale, a new service that focuses on proof of performance metrics from Nielsen, linked to the data beyond broadcast that stations already collect from the internet, social media, viewer services and education departments. Through staff training and building data-based narratives, Locale seeks to connect a station, its programming, and audiences together in relationships that create value in numerous ways. These can be monetizing audiences or building a compelling case for public broadcasting when the system is under political siege. PMC (*Public Media Company*) also is working to equip stations with strategies and tools for the next generation of television, ATSC 3.0. What we have reviewed here is merely the tip of the iceberg of this new industrial revolution that is now sweeping across the global economies of most nations. The key is to study the right problem(s) and forget about faster horses in a world that parses nanoseconds. We believe that local stations can adapt and thrive in a future that is admittedly hard to predict.

On an online article by Mr. Lynn Leahey, on 7 December 2017, said, that in every day, headlines remind us that the entire television ecosystem is experiencing a massive change. And yet, among the layoffs and mergers, local broadcast television is having a renaissance. By local broadcast, I mean all the channels you can receive in your city by using an antenna, often as many as 60-100 channels. These typically include 8-10 major networks, such as NBC and Univision, and hundreds of independent stations featuring music videos and programming in a myriad of languages, all serving local communities across the country. Antenna-TV uses a wonderful public national asset called the public airwaves, some people think are every bit as precious as our national parks.

So, what is changing? Audiences are increasingly demanding more from their viewing experience, from more high-quality content, greater choice, and convenience. And for the first time ever, we have the technology that has the potential to satisfy these demands for years to come. But it's been a long road to get here. Thirty years ago, the only way to access TV was through antenna-TV, giving us 10 to 15 channels over-the-air for free. We then decided what to watch either by "channel surfing" or using the TV guide magazine we bought at the grocery store (i.e. local newspapers). In the 80s and 90s, cable systems began offering a low-cost way to get better reception of local channels, particularly UHF stations. Soon, new cable-only channels started to appear, and households started paying for TV to receive a bundle of both cable channels (not available by antenna) and a subset of the antenna TV channels. Cable companies were later joined by satellite and phone companies to offer such cable-bundles, and by 10 or so years ago such a Pay TV cable-bundle was used by about 85% of all households with about 10% using antennas. More recently, the web/internet has become capable of distributing high-quality video, and a third way to watch TV blossomed – streaming-video-on-demand (SVOD) services like Netflix, Sling TV & Hulu, not to mention new video sources like YouTube and Facebook-Live.

While cable was growing, the country began getting away from visiting local mom-and-pop stores and restaurants to large, national chains. But now the pendulum is swinging back to local services with farm-to-table movements, shop local initiatives, and back to local broadcast TV. Thanks to cord-cutting (indoor or outdoor antennas) and newly formed homes not paying for cable (who never paid cable bundles), cable-bundle homes are now down to about 77% of all homes even with the new cable-bundle services like Sling TV and YouTube TV and is projected to drop to 65% or less in homes within the next five years. This means about 40 million homes in the US will be 'cord-free' and will either watch antenna-TV or not receive any live-linear TV at all. Bet on the former. Antenna (free-to-air) sales have been booming the last couple years and Millennials are discovering the simple fun of antenna-TV. So why is this happening. Also, with YouTube, it can now be projected to any smart TV.

We all love the amazing new programming coming from the broadcast TV networks and the new suppliers like Netflix, Amazon, Hulu. 'Binge watching' has become the newest way to watch TV and the country is watching more 'TV programming' than ever before. The availability of SVOD services is one reason for cord cutting. But while we love binge watching, it is not a casual viewing experience. It must be planned and often feels like a commitment. Across the nation, communities are looking more and more to local services such as farm-to-table food shopping and local businesses are taking more pride in their local city and local neighborhoods. We now see how local and national complement each other. This is true for TV too. Local broadcast is 'farm-to-table' TV as it not only has national network programming but local news on those network stations and many purely local, independent stations. Stations cater to local bilingual households which like both English and foreign language TV. And antenna-TV often has better picture quality than cable or internet TV.

So, what is the result?

1. Millennials and others are discovering the casual fun of channel surfing to discover new programs and be entertained without the commitment of binge watching. How about just a little TV before bed or while in the DMV line.

2. While the web has become a major source for news, more people see that live local news is a critical piece too, especially for timely critical information. Yes, Millennials are realizing this too.

3. TV stations are adding more interesting broadcast TV channels featuring more than just reruns and serving specific audiences with lifestyle content or science fiction and yes, once again, it is Millennials are discovering it all.

4. Businesses are also realizing the public airwaves and broadcast are valuable resources that complement the Internet. It is obvious that if one million households in Chicago are watching the Super Bowl, a broadcast signal is much more efficient and

practical than one million separate high bandwidth internet streams. Not long from now, the local broadcast infrastructure will be used to deliver data to devices all over the community (so-called internet of things, IOT), and sending the same data to many phones and laptops at the same time.

So local television broadcast TV and broadcasting is not going away soon, and probably never will. By my estimates, it will likely rise from 10% of households 10 years ago to 25%+ 10 years from now, particularly as it gets modernized via smartphone apps that allow easy access to antenna-TV via smartphones, tablets and laptops. I suppose that is why, even though many smart folks think it is going the way of the "buggy-whip," the value of broadcast stations has not gone down much over the years and is currently getting stronger. Cable-bundles will still be a big part of TV but as audiences seek greater choice and control over their viewing, they are rediscovering local broadcast and its low-cost, and easy convenience. How fortunate we are to have antenna-TV as a terrific part of our buffet of video programming.

The YouTube Sensation

How to become a YouTube Sensation

In an article online from the creative blog, it tells you what the future will be with television broadcasting. Whether you're demonstrating the finer points of illustration or handholding viewers through a UI design tutorial, YouTube offers the perfect platform for sharing your talents with the world – and with 1.9 billion logged in monthly users, we really do mean the world. Over half of YouTube visitors use the site to work out how to do things they've not done before, so making your own videos is a great way to position yourself as an expert in your field, sell your work and bring in more clients. But how do you compete with the millions of other videos on the ever-growing behemoth that is YouTube? True, you could choose an alternative platform like Vimeo and access a smaller, niche audience. But you all probably want more than the basic membership, which will cost you money (YouTube is free) and you may not appear high in search results, as Google favors YouTube videos.

Then there's Instagram's IGTV, which launched in 2018 with huge promise but lags way behind YouTube, especially if you want to publish high quality, in-depth content and access viewers with longer attention spans. So, aside from getting the best video editing software, how can you make it big on YouTube, maximize your views and promote your work? Read on for some top tips from creatives doing just that How long (or short) are the most successful videos? Martin Perhiniak's channel Yes, I am a Designer has 174, 000 subscribers and his most viewed video (above), which has been watched over 2.3 million times) is 40 minutes long. "In the case of educational videos, longer videos will attract more views as people will expect a more thorough explanation and more value," says Perhiniak. Fryer believes the ideal length depends on the subject matter. "I've had better results splitting longer videos into series. Around 15–20 minutes works best for most subject matters," he says. "But," he continues, "the real answer is: as short as possible without skipping key information." If a video is too short, people can feel short-changed or miss vital parts of the process.

Also bear in mind that 70 per cent of time spent on YouTube is watching content that the YouTube algorithm recommends. The algorithm prefers longer videos to keep people on the platform, so the longer you can keep users engaged, the better it is for your exposure. To grow views and followers, you need to build an interactive community around your content. "Try to be as personal as possible and respond to comments, queries, etc, inside and outside of YouTube," advises Fryer. Calls to action encourage people to engage and it pays to be bold. "Ask them questions, tell them to comment and like the video if they find it useful," says Perhiniak. "In some cases, it is better to pick a controversial topic than something safe as it will get more engagement but avoid click-bait videos. These can bring in a lot of views but won't help to grow your channel."

The Fight for the Future of YouTube

The video giant's recent travails underscore a basic question: How "neutral" should social-media platforms try to be?

Earlier this year, executives at YouTube began mulling, once again, the problem of online speech. On grounds of freedom of expression and ideological neutrality, the platform has long allowed users to upload videos endorsing noxious ideas, from conspiracy theories to neo-Nazism. Now it wanted to reverse course. "There are no sacred cows," Susan Wojcicki, the C.E.O. of YouTube, reportedly told her team. Wojcicki had two competing goals: she wanted to avoid accusations of ideological bias while also affirming her company's values. In the course of the spring, YouTube drafted a new policy that would ban videos trafficking in historical "denialism" (of the Holocaust, 9/11, Sandy Hook) and "supremacist" views (lauding the "white race," arguing that men were intellectually superior to women). YouTube planned to roll out its new policy as early as June. In May, meanwhile, it started preparing for Pride Month, turning its red logo rainbow-colored and promoting popular L.G.B.T.Q. video producers on Instagram.

On May 30th, Carlos Maza, a media critic at Vox, upended these efforts. In a Twitter thread that quickly went viral, Maza argued that the company's publicity campaign belied its lax enforcement of the content and harassment policies it had already put in place. Maza posted a video supercut of bigoted insults that he'd received from Steven Crowder, a conservative comedian with nearly four million YouTube followers; the insults focused on Maza's ethnicity and sexual orientation. When Crowder mentioned Maza in a video, his fans piled on; last year, Maza's cell phone was bombarded with hundreds of texts from different numbers which read "debate steven crowder." Maza said that he'd reported the behavior to YouTube's content moderators' numerous times, and that they had done nothing.

On Twitter and his YouTube channel, Crowder insisted that, in labelling Maza a "lispy queer" and a "token Vox gay-athiest sprite," he had been trying to be funny. Maza's supporters, meanwhile, shared screenshots of ads that had run before Crowder's videos, suggesting that, because YouTube offers popular video producers a cut of ad revenue, the company had implicitly condoned Crowder's messages. YouTube said it would investigate. A week later, it tweeted that Crowder had not violated its community guidelines in any of the videos that Maza highlighted. The next day, it announced its new policy, which included a warning that the company would no longer share ad revenue with YouTubers who repeatedly brushed up against its rules. Then it announced that Crowder would be cut off from the platform's ad dollars.

The news made no one happy. Maza said that he wanted Crowder's channel removed completely; conservatives, including the Republican senator Ted Cruz, complained about censorship. YouTube employees, siding with Maza, began denouncing their bosses on Twitter and in the press. "It's a classic move from a comms playbook," Micah Schaffer, a technology adviser who wrote YouTube's first community guidelines, told me. "Like, 'Hey, can we move up that launch to change the news cycle?' Instead, it made it worse. It combined into a Voltron of bad news." (A YouTube spokesperson said that the launch date was not in response to any individual event.) Former colleagues deluged Schaffer, who had left the company in 2009, with bewildered e-mails and texts. (A typical subject line: "WTF is Going on at YouTube?") Sitting in a dentist's office, he started typing a response on his phone, trying to lay out what he thought had gone wrong at the company.

Schaffer told me that hate speech had been a problem on YouTube since its earliest days. Dealing with it used to be fairly straightforward. YouTube was founded, in 2005, by Chad Hurley, Steve Chen, and Jawed Karim, who met while working at PayPal. At first, the site was moderated largely by its co-founders; in 2006, they hired a single, part-time moderator. The company removed videos often, rarely encountering pushback. In the intervening thirteen years, a lot has changed. "YouTube has the scale of the entire Internet," Sundar Pichai, the C.E.O. of Google, which owns YouTube, told Axios last month. The site now attracts a monthly audience of two billion people and employs thousands of moderators. Every minute, its users upload five hundred hours of new video. The technical, social, and political challenges of moderating such a system are profound. They raise fundamental questions not just about YouTube's business but about what social-media platforms have become and what they should be.

Perhaps because of the vast scale at which most social platforms operate, proposed solutions to the problem of online hate speech tend to be technical in nature. In theory, a platform might fine-tune its algorithms to deemphasize hate speech and conspiracy theories. But, in practice, this is harder than it sounds. Some overtly hateful users may employ language and symbols that clearly violate a site's community guidelines—but so-called borderline content, which dances at the edge of provocation, is harder to detect and draws a broad audience. Machine-learning systems struggle to tell the difference between actual hate speech and content that describes or contests it. (After YouTube announced its new policies, the Southern Poverty Law Center complained that one of its videos, which was meant to document hate speech, had been taken down.) Some automated systems use metadata—information about how often a user posts, or about the number of comments that a post gets in a short period of time—to flag toxic content without trying to interpret it. But this sort of analysis is limited by the way that content bounces between platforms, obscuring the full range of interactions it has provoked.

Tech companies have hired thousands of human moderators to make nuanced decisions about speech. YouTube also relies on anonymous outside "raters" to evaluate videos and help train its recommendations systems. But the flood of questionable posts is overwhelming and sifting through it can take a psychological toll. Earlier this year, YouTube described its efforts to draw more heavily on user feedback—survey responses, likes and dislikes—to help identify "quality" videos. And yet, in a 2016 white paper, the company's own engineers wrote that such metrics aren't very useful; the problem is that, for many videos, "explicit feedback is extremely sparse" compared to "implicit" signals, such as what users click on or how long they watch a video. Teen-agers who use YouTube more than any other kind of social media, often respond to surveys in mischievous ways.

Business challenges compound the technical ones. In a broad sense, any algorithmic change that dampens user engagement could work against YouTube's business model. Netflix, which is YouTube's chief rival in online video, can keep subscribers streaming by licensing or crafting addictive content; YouTube, by contrast, relies on user-generated clips, strung together by an automated recommendation engine. Programmers are always tweaking the system and the company is reluctant to disclose details. Still, a 2018 white paper outlined the general principle at that time: once someone starts watching a video, the engine is designed to "dig into a topic more deeply," luring the viewer down the proverbial rabbit hole. Many outside researchers argue that this system, which helped drive YouTube's engagement growth, also amplified hate speech and conspiracy theories on the platform. As the engine dug deeper, it risked making unsavory suggestions: unearth enough videos about the moon landing and some of them may argue that it was faked.

YouTube's Plans for 10 More Years of Video Domination

YouTube office is filled with its history. Inside the San Bruno, California, headquarters, about 45 minutes from the Googleplex in Mountain View, there is a YouTube video on every screen. Over here, the Smarter Every Day guys talk about the brain-bending backwards bicycle. Over there, Rick Astley promises he is never going to let you down. (YouTube's employees work in a semi-permanent state of Rick Roll.) On a table in one of the office's many kitchens, there's a pile of remotes for Google TV devices underneath a handwritten "FREE" sign. And of course, the red play button is everywhere you look big doorways, small desk ornaments. The conference rooms are named after YouTube phenomena: Double Rainbow, It is a Trap, Dos Equis Guy, and on and on and on. Inside the Lolcats conference room, VP of product management Matthew Glotzbach is describing the future of YouTube. He envisions an app so good, an algorithm so perfect, that it knows exactly what you want to watch at any given time. You wake up in the morning and catch up on the news while you get ready. Then, throughout the day, YouTube shows you shorter videos when you are waiting in line or in the bathroom: maybe some gadget reviews, or the best Jimmy Fallon bit you missed last night. At night, you come home, and use Chromecast to watch a movie or an episode of *Video Game High School* on your TV. YouTube wants to be more than a search engine for video. It wants to be the future, a perfect blend of TV and the internet, where everything is on demand but there is always something on. A decade after its debut, YouTube is a behemoth. It is become *the* place for video online. Three hundred hours of video are uploaded every minute, and it has well over a billion users worldwide. It's spawned a crop of celebrities, real honest-to-goodness famous people. It is by some measures the world's second-largest search engine. And it has pioneered entirely new ways of creating and consuming video.

Video was ascendant in the last decade, and it is going to be inescapable in the next one. YouTube cannot relax, though. Not yet, not ever. New challengers—everyone from Facebook and Snapchat to Vimeo and Vessel—are eyeing its talent and ready to poach its viewers. Absolutely everyone is coming for its advertisers, who have untold billions to spend and serious demands about where it goes. YouTube needs to prove it can turn impossibly huge view counts into actual, real profit. The plan? Make sure everyone on the planet can get online, and on YouTube. They're working with carriers and ISPs to figure out how to stream to anyone no matter what their connection looks like. Then, get so good at showing them videos they like that they'll never want to turn off. That requires teaching their computers what is inside your videos, what videos you want to see, and what formats and video types are coming next. The video industry moves fast, and YouTube must stay faster. Simple, right?

Just Press Play

Buffering is the dirtiest word at YouTube. The people who work there say it a lot, always with a sort of cringing, pained look. It's like they're remembering a bad breakup or just woke up to a crushing hangover. "There was some stat that we used to have that was like, if the YouTube buffer symbol was a webpage, it would be the third most popular website in the world," Glotzbach says. Then he hastily adds: "Not now, though!"

The Future of YouTube

May 1, 2019

If you ask Justin Khoe, a former youth minister with an endlessly enthusiastic attitude, there is something slightly disturbing about the experience of running a YouTube channel. "It's a very weird phenomenon," he told me recently. "When you are starting a channel and you get 100 subscribers, you're really stoked. But it's amazing how you can be less happy with twice as many followers than you were with that first 100." Khoe runs *That Christian Vlogger,* creating videos with titles like "Waiting for God SUCKS!!!" and "The SURPRISING truth about why Jesus came to Earth." Getting enough views can be stressful in two different ways. Because it's Khoe's full-time job, it needs to bring in enough money to pay his half of the expenses for the home he shares with his wife. At the same time, he said, there is a danger that his earnest hope of reaching more people with his faith can turn into a bottomless hunger for clicks. "The higher you climb, the more likely you are to identify with those metrics," Khoe said. "If you're not careful, it can be something that kind of robs the joy from you for why you started the thing in the first place." That is not just a problem for earnest religious YouTubers. Across the vast array of YouTube channels, from goofy pranksters to style gurus, creators face the same tension between creative fulfillment and objective measures of success.

Streaming boxes and other devices

CATV (originally "community antenna television," now often "community access or public television") is more commonly known as "cable TV." In addition to bringing television programs to those millions of people throughout the world who are connected to a community antenna, cable TV is an increasingly popular way to interact with the World Wide Web and other new forms of multimedia information and entertainment services.

In conclusion, public television broadcasters being comprised of 170 licensees operating more than 350 public television stations across

America and serving more than 98 percent of the American people. As stated before, about half of these licensees are nonprofit community foundations. The rest are State, university and local school district licensees. All are locally owned, locally operated, and locally oriented in their programming and community services, and all share a mission of serving everyone, everywhere, every day for free – including in places where no model for commercial success exists. However, free to view, it's not so much free to gain in-home access if their being broadcasted on local cable systems. Therefore, besides the continued high costs of cable and satellite television services are changing the viewing platforms because of these new streaming devices and services.

With the invention of streaming boxes such as YouTube TV, ROKU, Smart Stream, Apple TV, and other steaming devices that broadcast local, state, national and international TV channels. More and more of the public are using these stream boxes to cut the high cost of bundles by cable and telephone companies that provide home phone, cable and internet services. Community television broadcasters (CTV) may not have a spot on these streaming devices unless a national advocate organization addresses this issue with the companies that provide streaming services. There are a few local community television broadcasters that either stream live or have a library on their website that can be watch using the internet.

These new streaming devices will dominate the media industry and will become a mainstay to most homes nationwide and internationally. As most inventions become available on the market the public will adapt as well as the television broadcast industries will also adapt to their public's desires on the method on which their audiences view their media. What I think would be a cool way to watch television is to be interactive in what we view. Watch for hologram rooms to be the next generation of media viewing. Stream network TV shows without a cable subscription with these apps:

1. CTV Go. The CTV Go app (available for iOS and Android) gives you on-demand access to a wide variety of shows, including hit series from ABC. ...

2. Global Go. For CBS shows, turn to the Global Go app (available for iOS and Android). ...
3. City Video.

On 8 Nov 2005, on an online article, a proposed legislation may affect the future of Public-Access Television. One recent afternoon, in a small brownstone dwarfed by the shine and sprawl of the nearby Time Warner Center in Midtown Manhattan, Joel Igartua got ready for his close-up. The 18-year-old high school senior was honing his interview skills and mastering video camera basics to make public service announcements for Manhattan Neighborhood Network, a public-access television station. "People should have the right to make their own shows," Mr. Igartua said. "TV is powerful. Everyone watches TV."

For every hour of "Desperate Housewives" on ABC, the nation's 3,000 public-access television channels present dozens of hours of local school board meetings, Little League games and religious services. Not to mention programs like "The Great Grown-Up Spelling Bee," a spelling bee for adults that raises money for the Kalamazoo, Mich., public library, and "Fruta Extrena," a bilingual gay talk show in New York City. Now, though, the future of the channels deemed "electronic soapboxes" in 1972 by the Federal Communications Commission is uncertain, as proposed legislation about how the telecommunications industry is regulated winds its way through Congress.

The main concern for public-access advocates is that the law preserve the ability of municipalities to negotiate franchise agreements for cable television. Those agreements pay for the public-access programs and allow municipalities to determine how many channels they want and allow public access programmers like Manhattan Neighborhood Network to train nonprofit groups to produce their own shows. The proposed legislation varies in its specifics, but several bills aim to allow more video-services competition -- easing the way for telephone companies to compete for the franchises -- and minimize regulations for franchises. Advocates of the legislation say that the fears of the demise of public access are exaggerated and that some local control of franchises is written into the bills.

Currently, most cable franchise agreements include a franchise fee paid by cable providers for using city property, putting millions of dollars in city coffers, some of which can be used for public-access channels. Some agreements also provide explicit financing and support for the community's use of the cable system. Public, educational and government -- or "PEG" -- access channels tend to be uneven in their quality and production values. But, say advocates, these shows are not meant to sell products or just entertain, but to mirror community interests and needs. "There has to be some portion of the system open to public use, which has public revenue supporting it," Anthony T. Riddle, executive director of the Washington-based Alliance for Community Media, said of his advocacy of public access. The group represents 1,000 media centers nationwide.

Yesterday, to take advantage of election eve, thousands of public-access channels nationwide were scheduled to show one minute of video snow simultaneously to protest the legislative proposals, beginning at 9 p.m., Eastern time. The alliance is joined by the National League of Cities and the United States Conference of Mayors in opposing any bill that would strip local control of cable franchises. Public-access advocates are appealing to politicians and to the public to hear their case.

The cable business has $60 billion in revenue annually, and last year cable operators paid $2.4 billion in franchise fees, according to the National Cable and Telecommunications Association, the cable industry's principal trade association.

Under federal law, cities can collect a franchise fee that is up to 5 percent of the gross revenue generated from the delivery of cable services. With 33,000 local cable franchises across the country, telephone companies are now pressuring the federal government for speedier access to franchises and fewer restrictions. In Texas recently, SBC and Verizon got that state to set up a uniform clearing-house approach, meaning that these companies can apply to the state for franchises and do not have to negotiate agreements with each municipality separately. "One of the big questions is, Is there a place for public interest in our media policy, or is it one size fits all?" said Rick Junger, the director of community media at Manhattan Neighborhood Network.

The National Cable and Telecommunications Association has not weighed in on any specifics of the proposed laws because it is too early, said a spokesman for the association, Rob Stoddard. The organization's concern, he said, is that any new rules on franchises apply to all video providers, whether they are traditional cable providers or telephone companies.

What advocates hope is not lost in all the fights over politics and technology is their idea of public access as a First Amendment right, especially for people and towns underrepresented on television. The local franchise agreements, they said, have provided a tried and true mechanism to handle customer complaints, determine local programming needs and deliver the money to produce those programs.

Mr. Riddle said that the groups he represents produced 20,000 hours of new programs a week, using 1.2 million volunteers and 250,000 community groups in any given year. That's more programming, he added, than the broadcast networks combined. "It's where we turn for a sense of self," Laurie Cirivello, executive director of the Community Media Center of Santa Rosa, said of the four access channels in her Northern California community of 150,000. The channels feature locally produced shows like "Mrs. Twizzleton's Magic Garden," a children's program with a local psychologist as host, and a number of Spanish-language shows. Ms. Cirivello noted that Santa Rosa, near San Francisco, has no local television stations.

Legislators say their bills are needed because the current telecommunication laws did not foresee the Internet explosion, or new video technology like telephone service over the Internet, and interactive television.

The Video Choice Act, introduced in the House by Marsha Blackburn, Republican of Tennessee, has been referred to the House Energy and Commerce Committee. The Senate version, introduced by Gordon Smith, Republican of Oregon, and Jay Rockefeller, Democrat of West Virginia, has been referred to the Senate Commerce, Science and Transportation Committee. In the Senate, a bill introduced by John Ensign, Republican of Nevada, which covers a broader range of telecommunications issues, is known as the Broadband Investment and Consumer Choice Act.

"This legislation allows consumers -- not government bureaucrats -- to choose the best services at the best prices," Senator Ensign said in an e-mail message. The Ensign bill, now also in the Senate Commerce, Science and Transportation Committee, has drawn the most fire from opponents, who say the House and Senate versions of the Video Choice Act are more flexible in their language.

"It is just flat wrong to say we eliminate public, educational and government channels," Senator Ensign said. "Our bill specifically requires video providers to carry up to four PEG channels."

He said his bill did not eliminate the 5 percent franchise fee. It extends it, he said, to new video providers and also has an entire section protecting the ability of state and local governments to manage their rights of way.

Representative Blackburn said that her bill was intended to create more affordable video options and more diversity in programming. "My bill seeks to keep limitations and regulations to a minimum in order to encourage an active, growing marketplace rather than the atrophied one we have right now," she said in an e-mail message.

But public-access advocates argue that these are empty words and that questions remain, including those concerning how franchise fees are defined and who oversees the collection of right-of-way revenue. Senator Ensign's aides acknowledged that the definition of "revenue" for franchise fees was still debatable. Whether revenue from purchases on a home shopping channel should be included, as they currently are, is one question that has to be answered, an aide to Senator Ensign said. The Ensign bill also caps the number of access channels at four in each municipality, although some big cities already have more. New York City, for example, has nine PEG channels.

Ralph Engelman, the chairman of the journalism department at Long Island University's Brooklyn campus, said, "The whole concept is a somewhat radical, democratic vision -- giving ordinary citizens access to the most persuasive communications medium that exists." He added: "It's incredibly diverse, and it's very raw. It's probably a better reflection of what our society is than mainstream television."

The personalities from public access sometimes even make it onto mainstream television. RuPaul, the cross-dressing entertainer, kicked off his career in 1982 on a weekly public-access show in Atlanta called "The American Music Show."

On 14 August 2014, in an online article "*Saving Community Access*". Community or public access television broadcasters were concered about their future. While most of us are aware of community access television — those cable channels that are reserved for local government and public access programming — few people recognize what an important resource this is for communities throughout the nation. More than 3,000 Public, Educational and Governmental (PEG) cable channels are operating around the country, offering information about everything from local city council hearings to community events, and featuring community-generated programs from cooking shows to local musical talent. Particularly in underserved urban, suburban and rural communities, the PEG channels offer a vital community connection.

But these community channels are facing serious threats — not simply from the funding crisis faced by all municipalities, but also because of a loophole in a 40-year-old federal law that could easily be closed. Not to get too deep into the legislative weeds, but the 1984 Cable Act, which governs this area, limited the use of PEG funds separate from and in addition to franchise fees to capital improvements, but not for staff or operations to run studios. As anyone who has tried to run an arts or broadcast organization knows, having the facilities is worthless without someone to operate them. Community access media is no different.

Fortunately, there is a growing movement afoot to save community access by closing this loophole. "Many organizations including the National Association of Telecommunications Officers and Administrators (NATOA), the National Alliance for Media Arts and Culture (NAMAC) and FreePress to name a few, have devoted time and effort to advocate for the continued support of community media," said Keri Stokstad, Alliance for Community Media Board Chair and Executive Director of Pasadena Media in Pasadena, California. "It is imperative that we honor the intention of the Cable Act to ensure resources are allocated to support local content creation."

In fact, beginning later this week, the Conference of Mayors, meeting in Dallas, will consider a resolution that would call on Congress to amend the Cable Act and thus assure the future of community access television. "Community access is vital to the future of towns and cities across the nation," said Michael Wassenaar, the public policy advocate for the Alliance for Community Media. "It provides a voice for millions of underserved Americans, and is critical to the free and open flow of information in our society." Hopefully, the Congress will see the wisdom in fixing the loopholes in current law and restore the promise of community access to all Americans.

On 15 February 2019, an online aricle, local community cable television broadcasters show concerns about the rullings of Federal Communications Commission about their future with contracts with cable companies. Since the mid-1980s, community cable TV production crews, mostly volunteers, have been bringing local news, high school sports, parades, government meetings and other city and town events to viewers' living rooms. But the quantity and quality of those programs is now being threatened by a rule change being considered by the Federal Communications Commission.

Joe Catalano sat in the Quincy Access Television station waiting for the show he hosts, "Currently in Quincy," to go live with an interview of new Quincy College President Michael Bellotti, the former Norfolk County sheriff.

Behind a glass wall, three volunteers and the show's director, Mike Jarvie, were ready to roll cameras and cue up public service announcements for Quincy organizations, along with highlights of Quincy High School basketball games and a clip the station captured of Quincy Mayor Thomas Koch announcing a new initiative. Jarvie pressed a button to start the intro and counted down: "Three, two, one. Go, Joe."

Up and down the South Shore and across the country, community television shows like Catalano's are using cable company channels, studios and equipment on a daily basis to bring local news, high school sports, parades, government meetings and other community events to viewers' living rooms.

Local programming is supported by franchise fees that cable companies pay cities and towns – capped by the Federal Communications Commission at 5 percent of the company's gross revenue – and by free cable company channels to carry the programs and cable service to schools and government buildings negotiated as "in-kind benefits" in licensing agreements with towns.

Advocates of local programming say both forms of support are needed to maintain the variety and quality of community cable TV. But the FCC is now poised to consider a rule change that would allow cable companies to use the value of some in-kind benefits to reduce franchise fees. And that, advocates say, could be the ruin of community television. "This is an existential threat to local access," Milton Selectman Mike Zullas said. "When you open the door like that, you're going to threaten the whole of the franchise fees."

Cable television service made its debut on the South Shore in the early 1980s, with companies competing to win franchise license agreements in cities and towns. As sweeteners, companies promised to provide local access television studios, equipment and professional staff to train volunteers who wanted to produce their own programming. Companies also promised to pay franchise fees that cover operating costs.

Municipal leaders and others predict that allowing cable companies to reduce franchise fees by the value of in-kind donations would cut spending for local programs by 30 to 70 percent, a loss of $100,000 to as much as $500,000 a year, depending on the community.

That could spell the end of at least some government meeting broadcasts and programs highlighting small-town news that might not find its way to regional newspapers or Boston news stations.

"The loss of access television will make it especially difficult for non-headlining information to be shared with city and town residents," Mark Crosby, government access coordinator for Quincy Access Television, said.

Weymouth Mayor Robert Hedlund said community television is even more important as newspapers cut back on municipal meeting coverage.

"Having broadcasted meetings is becoming more essential, and public access has helped fill the void," he said.

Advocates of the rule change say cable subscribers ultimately foot the bill for community television, and that current regulations make it easy for cities and towns to ask for in-kind benefits that have nothing to do with local cable programming. As an example, a New York community's request for a video hookup for a Christmas celebration included money for wildflower seeds, reports the fiscally conservative think tank Citizens Against Government Waste, which supports the FCC rule change.

"It's about preventing the outlier municipalities from asking cable companies to pay for extraneous costs," said Deborah Collier, director of tech policy for the think tank in Washington, D.C. "This isn't going to affect public access television."

The FCC says the rule change would prevent cities and towns from extracting in-kind benefits that are unrelated to cable programming and eliminate "unreasonable barriers" for new companies trying to enter the market.

But Mike Bradley, a Minnesota-based municipal lawyer who works on cable licenses throughout the country, said the idea that in-kind benefits pose a barrier to new companies entering the market is "pure nonsense."

"Cable operators have been paying franchise fees in the same way since well before even the Cable Act was passed in 1984," Bradley said. "The Cable Act already allows the cable operator to fully recover all of its franchising costs through its rates."

An FCC spokeswoman declined to comment on the proposed rule change or provide a timeline for when it might be approved. The FCC solicited comments on the proposal through December.

Comcast, one of the major cable providers on the South Shore, did not answer questions about how it would value in-kind contributions to offset franchise fees or whether it supports the FCC rule change. In an email, a spokesman did say the company invested $12.9 million worth of cash and in-kind contributions in Massachusetts communities in 2017.

Verizon, which also holds cable license agreements in the region, declined to comment.

People involved with cable community television on the South Shore said there is a great deal of uncertainty about the future of local programming in part because the effect of the FCC's rule change, if approved, is unclear.

"There's not a list saying, 'These are going to be the things we're going to deduct and here's the cost of them,'" Marshfield Community Television executive director Jonathan Grabowski said. "They haven't decided. Is it going to be the fiber that runs from my studio to town hall so we can broadcast the selectmen's meeting live? And no one knows the cost of that. No one knows the cost of putting our channels on Comcast and Verizon, to have them on the cable box. There's so many unknowns."

Wesley Rea, executive director of Braintree Community Access & Media, said he worries that if the FCC rule change is approved, cable companies would be able to charge for channels that carry local programs against the franchise fee, or that Comcast, which still has a service facility in Braintree, would use some of its value as an offset.

"What's the value of a retail business in the town of Braintree?" Rea said. "A big concern is that they'll charge back the value of a channel. No one has said what that will cost. ... That would wipe us out."

Advocates of local cable TV say it's not only programming that's at risk, but education. Local studios often take on interns and volunteers and partner with public high schools and colleges to teach television production.

Grabowski, the Marshfield television executive director, said his studio collaborates with Marshfield High School on a communications program and has a paid intern program for students. Quincy Access Television teaches interns from area colleges.

Grace Buscher, a Quincy resident and Quincy Access Television board member, said it's important to have local voices on television.

"Public access TV is what gives the individual in a town or city the ability to have a voice," Buscher, a volunteer producer for 17 years, said. "I have a number of programs that I have run over the years. Some of them have been successful and some of them have been downright failures ... but (local television) is one of the only places you can come in and put on whatever you want to."

Bradley, the Minnesota lawyer, says he hopes the wait for an FCC ruling is a long one.

"The FCC doesn't have to take any action. And frankly, I hope they don't, because I think they're absolutely wrong," he said. "So there's no set timetable. They could take months, they could take years. And they could just let it sit there forever."

In conclusion. With the Federal Communication Commission, US Congress and local municipalities are unsure of the legislation rights of public television broadcaster's future. It's seems logical that either the internet, streaming boxes or YouTube would be the ideal platforms for local public television broadcasters the sustain this sector of television broadcasters in the United States and around the world.

REFERENCES

A

"A Small History of the Open Channel Dortmund." Offener Kanal Dortmund. (Nov. 12, 1999). Retrieved May 11, 2000, from the World Wide Web: http://www.ins.net/offener-kanal-dortmund/english/history.htm

B

Baldwin, Thomas F. & McVoy, D. Stevens. *Cable communication.* Englewood Cliffs, NJ: Prentice Hall, 1988.

Beck, Kirsten. *Cultivating the Wasteland: Can Cable Put the Vision Back in TV?* New York, NY: American Council for the Arts, 1983

Bretz, Rudy. *Handbook for Producing Educational and Public-Access Programs for Cable Television.* Englewood Cliffs, NJ: Educational Technology Publications, 1976.

Britannica
https://www.britannica.com/art/television-in-the-United-States.

C

"Cable television." *The Network Project, Notebook Number Five.* New York, NY: June 1973.

Community Television:
https://en.wikipedia.org/wiki/Community_television

Caraway, Sylvester Jr. Community Television Broadcasting in Australia *"The Development of Commercialism"*, Ph.D. thesis

Caraway Jr, Sylvester. Understanding Public Broadcasting Services, Ronald E. McNair graduate program, thesis

Carpenter-Huffman, Polly & Kletter, Richard C. & Yin, Robert K. *Cable Television, Developing Community Services*. New York, NY: Crane, Russak & Company, Inc., 1974.

Crandall, Robert W. & Furchtgott-Roth, Harold. *Cable TV: Regulation or Competition?* Washington, D.C.: The Brookings Institute, 1996.

Creative Blog; https://www.creativebloq.com/features/how-to-become-a-youtube-sensation; Published: June 20, 2019

D

Daily Jstor; https://daily.jstor.org/how-youtube-is-shaping-the-future-of-work/ May 1, 2019

Denver Area Educational Telecommunications Consortium, Inc., et al. v. Federal Communications Commission et al. (United States Supreme Court case number unknown).

Dove, Laurie L., Who runs public access TV channels, https://entertainment.howstuffworks.com/how-does-public-access-tv-work.htm

E

https://eprints.qut.edu.au/15829/

Engelman, Ralph. "Origins of Public Access Cable Television," 1966-1972. Columbia, SC: *Journalism Monographs*. Number 123, Oct. 1990.

F

FCC https://www.patriotledger.com/news/20190215/will-fcc-rule-change-ruin-community-cable-tv

FCC v. Midwest Video Corp., 440 U.S. 689.

Forbes, Dorothy & Layng, Sanderson. *New Communicators: A Guide to Community Programming.*Communications Press, Inc. by arrangement with the Canadian Cable Television Association, 1977.

G

Gillmor, Dan Beyond Broadcast: Future of Public Access TV, http://citmedia.org/blog/2007/02/21/beyond-broadcast-future-of-public-access-tv/

Feb 21ˢᵗ, 2007

Gillespie, Gilbert. *Public Access Cable Television in the United States and Canada.* New York: Praeger Publishers, 1975.

H

"História do Canal." Canal Comunitário de Porto Alegre. (March 2000). Retrieved May 11, 2000, from the World Wide Web: http://www.canalcomunitario.com.br/historia_2.html

Hollins, Timothy. *Beyond Broadcasting: Into the Cable Age.* London: Published for the Broadcasting Research Unit by BFI Publishing, 1984.

Hollowell, Mary Louise (ed.). *Cable/Broadband Communications Book, Vol. 2*, 1980-1981. Washington, D.C.: Communications Press, Inc., 1980.

Hollowell, Mary Louise (ed.). *Cable/Broadband Communications Book, Vol. 3*, 1982-1983. Washington, D.C.: Communications Press, Inc., 1983.

I

J

K

L

Lautenshlager, Scott & Price, John. "Controversy Brews over Airing of Bangert Tape," *Eau Claire Leader-Telegram*, August 16, 1983

Leahey, Lynn. The Future of the Local Broadcast TV, http://www. cynopsis.com/cyncity/the-future-of-the-local-broadcast-tv/December 7, 2017

"Legislação." Canal Comunitário de Porto Alegre. (March 2000). Retrieved May 11, 2000, from the World Wide Web: http://www. canalcomunitario.com.br/legislacao.html

M

https://moody.utexas.edu/sites/default/files/stein_3.pd
http://mediashift.org/2008/12/public-access-tv-fights-for-relevance-in-the-youtube-age352/
Museum: www.museum.tv.eotv/publicaccess.thm.

N

National Cable Television Association. *Over the cable*. Washington, D.C.: National Cable Television Association, 1974.

New York University / Tisch School of the Arts / Maurice Kanbar Institute of Film and Television / People / Undergraduate. (May 11, 2000). Retrieved May 11, 2000, from the World Wide Web: http:// www.nyu.edu/tisch/filmtv/ind_people.html

New Yorker; https://www.newyorker.com/tech/annals-of-technology/ the-fight-for-the-future-of-youtube; 29 January 2019.

Newsweek, Jan. 3, 1972. (Cited in Engelman, 34.)

O

https://www.cynopsis.com/cyncity/the-future-of-the-local-broadcast-tv/(Elinor Rennie, 03 Dec 2008 03:50)

Oakland Post: http://www.oaklandpost.org/2016/10/10/future-local-public-access-television-stations/

P

PACT: "The History of Public Access Community Television in Eau Claire, Wisconsin." Cable 11, Public Access Community Television. (May 2000). Retrieved May 11, 2000, from the World Wide Web: http://www.cvctv.org/histo.htm

PEG: https://en.everybodywiki.com/List_of_public-access_TV_stations_in_the_United_States_(Delaware%E2%80%93Kentucky)

"Playboy Interview - Marshall McLuhan," March 1969. McLuhan Center on Global Communications. (January 2000). Retrieved May 11, 2000, from World Wide Web: http://www.mcluhanmedia.com/m_mcl_inter_pb_03.html

Proposed legislation my affect future public television access https://www.nytimes.com/2005/11/08/arts/television/proposed-legislation-may-affect-future-of-publicaccess.html

Q

R

Reed, Craigd, Executive Director (TRAC Media Services), David LeRoy, Co-Founder (TRAC Media Services), Judith LeRoy, Co-Founder (TRAC Media Services) and Vincent Curren, Principal(Breakthrough Public Media Consulting) Beyond-broadcast strategies key to survival of local public TV stations. February 28, 2017

Roberts, Jason. (October 1994). "Public Access: Fortifying the Electronic Soapbox," *Federal Communications Law Journal*. Vol. 47, No.

1. Retrieved May 11, 2000, from the World Wide Web: http://www. law.indiana.edu/fclj/pubs/v47/no1/roberts.html

S

Saving Community Access: https://www.huffpost.com/entry/ saving-community-access-t_b_5511363

"Series List: Newfoundland Project." National Film Board of Canada. (May 8, 2000). Retrieved May 11, 2000, from the World Wide Web: http://www.nfb.ca/FMT/E/seri/N/Newfoundland_Project.html

Shaffer, Wm. Drew & Wheelwright, Richard (editors for the National Federation of Local Cable Programmers). *Creating Original Programming for Cable TV.* Washington, D.C.: Communications Press, Inc., 1983.

Shamberg, Michael & Raindance Corporation. *Guerrilla Television.* New York: Holt, Rinehart and Winston of Canada, 1971. (Shamberg I = first part: "Meta-Manual." Shamberg II = second part: "Official Manual." Page numbers 3 through 37 duplicates in the two parts.)

T

The History of Access TV: http://www.tbcn.org/index.php?option= com_content&view=article&id=96&Itemid=280#:~:text=The%20 History%20of%20Public%20Access%20Television%20 HISTORY%20-,%28DCTV%29%2C%20but%20the%20 center%20failed%20two%20years%20later.

The History of Public Access TV; http://billolsonvideo.com/history-public-access-TV.html; Copyright 2000 by William D.S. Olson

The Global Village CAT. (April 23, 2000). Retrieved May 11, 2000, from the World Wide Web: http://www.openchannel.se/cat/links.htm

Host Lauren-Glenn Davitian: 10/06/2015, The Future of Public Access Television (Video) : https://www.cctv.org/watch-tv/programs/ future-public-access-television

U

V

W

Wired; https://www.wired.com/2015/05/youtube-future/ May 12, 2015

X

Y

Z

ADDITIONAL READING

Alvarez, Sally M. *Reclaiming the Public Sphere: A Study of Public Access Television Programming by the U.S.* Labor Movement. (Ph.D. dissertation, University of North Carolina, 1995).

Caraway, Sylvester Jr., *Community Television Broadcast in Australia.* The Development of Commercialism (Ph.D. dissertation, Griffith University, Nathan Campus, Queensland 2008).

Caraway, Sylvester Jr. *The Understanding of Public Broadcasting in the United States.* (Ronald E. McNair Graduate Honors at California State University, Sacramento, California 2001).

Frederiksen, H. Allan. *Community Access Video.* Menlo Park, California: Nowells, 1972.

Fuller, Linda K. *Community Television in the United States.* Westport, Connecticut: Greenwood Press, 1994. Source: https://www.questia.com/library/3854086/community-television-in-the-united-states-a-sourcebook

Kellner, Douglas. *Television and the Crisis of Democracy.* Boulder, Colorado: Westview Press, 1990.

Olson, W.D. Sherman (Bill), *THE HISTORY OF PUBLIC ACCESS TELEVISION,* 1 August 2002. Online: http://billolsonvideo.com/history-public-access-TV.html

Phillips, Mary Alice Mayer. *CATV: A History of Community Antenna Television.* Evanston, Illinois.: Northwestern University Press, 1972.

Ryan, Charlotte. *Prime-Time Activism*. Boston: South End Press, 1991.

Baldwin, Thomas F. & McVoy, D. Stevens. *Cable communication*. Englewood Cliffs, NJ: Prentice Hall, 1988.

Denver Area Educational Telecommunications Consortium, Inc., et al. v. Federal Communications Commission et al. (United States Supreme Court case number unknown).

Engelman, Ralph. "Origins of Public Access Cable Television," 1966-1972. Columbia, SC: *Journalism Monographs*. Number 123, Oct. 1990.

FCC v. Midwest Video Corp., 440 U.S. 689.

Gillespie, Gilbert. *Public Access Cable Television in the United States and Canada*. New York: Praeger Publishers, 1975.

The Global Village CAT. (April 23, 2000). Retrieved May 11, 2000, from the World Wide Web: http://www.openchannel.se/cat/links.htm

"História do Canal." Canal Comunitário de Porto Alegre. (March 2000). Retrieved May 11, 2000, from the World Wide Web: http://www.canalcomunitario.com.br/historia_2.html

Hollowell, Mary Louise (ed.). *Cable/Broadband Communications Book, Vol. 2*, 1980-1981. Washington, D.C.: Communications Press, Inc., 1980.

Hollowell, Mary Louise (ed.). *Cable/Broadband Communications Book, Vol. 3*, 1982-1983. Washington, D.C.: Communications Press, Inc., 1983.

Lautenshlager, Scott & Price, John. "Controversy Brews over Airing of Bangert Tape," *Eau Claire Leader-Telegram*, August 16, 1983

"Legislação." Canal Comunitário de Porto Alegre. (March 2000). Retrieved May 11, 2000, from the World Wide Web: http://www.canalcomunitario.com.br/legislacao.html

Newsweek, Jan. 3, 1972. (Cited in Engelman, 34.)

New York University / Tisch School of the Arts / Maurice Kanbar Institute of Film and Television / People / Undergraduate. (May 11, 2000). Retrieved May 11, 2000, from the World Wide Web: http://www.nyu.edu/tisch/filmtv/ind_people.html

PACT: "The History of Public Access Community Television in Eau Claire, Wisconsin." Cable 11, Public Access Community Television. (May 2000). Retrieved May 11, 2000, from the World Wide Web: http://www.cvctv.org/histo.htm

"Playboy Interview - Marshall McLuhan," March 1969. McLuhan Center on Global Communications. (January 2000). Retrieved May 11, 2000, from World Wide Web: http://www.mcluhanmedia.com/m_mcl_inter_pb_03.html

Roberts, Jason. (October 1994). "Public Access: Fortifying the Electronic Soapbox," *Federal Communications Law Journal*. Vol. 47, No. 1. Retrieved May 11, 2000, from the World Wide Web: http://www.law.indiana.edu/fclj/pubs/v47/no1/roberts.html

"Series List: Newfoundland Project." National Film Board of Canada. (May 8, 2000). Retrieved May 11, 2000, from the World Wide Web: http://www.nfb.ca/FMT/E/seri/N/Newfoundland_Project.html

Shamberg, Michael & Raindance Corporation. *Guerrilla Television*. New York: Holt, Rinehart and Winston of Canada, 1971. (Shamberg I = first part: "Meta-Manual." Shamberg II = second part: "Official Manual." Page numbers 3 through 37 duplicates in the two parts.)

"A Small History of the Open Channel Dortmund." Offener Kanal Dortmund. (Nov. 12, 1999). Retrieved May 11, 2000, from the World Wide Web: http://www.ins.net/offener-kanal-dortmund/english/history.htm

CPSIA information can be obtained
at www.ICGtesting.com
Printed in the USA
BVHW030921240521
607631BV00014B/1114/J

9 781637 284889